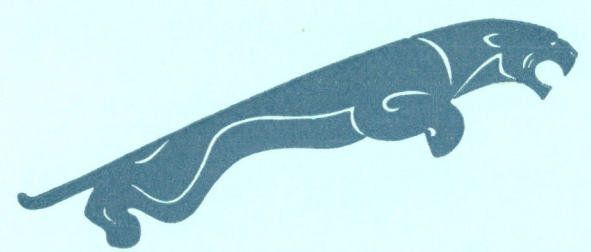

THE JAGUAR TRADITION

Nothing has brought the Jaguar Company more fame than the five victories at Le Mans. Here on the fifth and last occasion in 1957 when privately owned cars finished 1st, 2nd, 3rd, 4th and 6th, is Duncan Hamilton about to leave the pits.

THE JAGUAR TRADITION

MICHAEL FROSTICK

DALTON WATSON LTD
LONDON

First Published 1973

ISBN 0901564 117
Library of Congress Catalog Card Number 73-80223
© DALTON WATSON LTD.

Process Engravings by Star Illustration Works Ltd.

*Printed in England by the Lavenham Press Ltd.
for the publishers*
DALTON WATSON LTD.
76 Wardour Street, London W1V 4AN

Distributed in the U.S.A. by
MOTORBOOKS INTERNATIONAL
3501 Hennepin Avenue South
Minneapolis
Minnesota 55408

Author's Note

This is, of course, not the first book to be published on the subject of Sir William Lyons' Jaguar Company, its traditions and its acquisitions; but for all that there is good reason to include the marque in the Dalton Watson series which has already created a special place for itself in the motoring literature of cars for which enthusiasm runs high.

This enthusiasm for the motor car can hardly be thought of as a new idea, since from the Hon. C. S. Rolls onwards the idea has been rampant. And yet today, when the motor car as we have known it all these years must be nearing the end of its life, there is a new wave of enthusiasm quite beyond the conception of the early motorists — or even of those between the wars. Furthermore it is much more widespread.

In large measure this has been brought about by the Vintage Sports Car Club in Great Britain; and in other countries by those clubs which followed their lead. But nowadays it is the preoccupation with history, and with a particular marque, that seems to distinguish the enthusiast, and the cult is not limited to collectors of the *Grandes Marques,* or even to those with authentic vintage leanings; but encompasses all kinds of persons many of whom only have a love for, say, their third or fourth Jaguar. And yet there are limits, some makes have quite escaped any kind of real enthusiasm — and hardly seem to have deserved such a slight; while others with no great claim to merit have a kind of film star following.

Which brings us to the vexed question of what does make a collectors car, and what might merit a volume such as this. The VSCC are quite clear on the point; and their rules are too well known to call for either repetition or comment here; but for all their possible excellence they are not all embracing — for they ignore completely those cars made after the war — many of which are already becoming collectors items. Clearly it is not just a question of excellence — though few bad cars are collected, it is perhaps more a question of style, for in many cases appearance seems to outweigh mechanical virtue. Rarity has something to do with it, yet that does little to explain the popularity of the Jaguar, though the early SS models are certainly not be to seen on every street corner. Fashion changes too, for the Mark V was not all that prized in its day and yet is now of more than passing interest. The original XK120 and one would guess the XK140 Coupé are about to join the immortals, and quite rightly so, for they were always very special cars — but would you call a 1934 SSII special?

In some measure we have now found some sense in the American idea of a "Classic", for there is no doubt that not everyone who wants an "interesting" old car wants the mechanical uncertainties that so often go with it — nor does everyone's wife accept cheerfully the exposure to the elements that so many vintage men enjoy. There is something to be said for a collectors car that can be every-day transport. In fact there are no rules, one man's meat is still another man's poison; but while motoring persists, a love of cars will go with it and there are an increasing number of makes with their own very powerful following. Not the least among them being the Jaguar.

As with its companion volumes this does not set out to be the history of the firm, though within its pages the history must unfold, it does however offer the most comprehensive collection of photographs that author and publisher have been able to assemble; and in this respect at least is a definitive guide to what the cars looked like. Such a collection I hope may sometimes help to settle argument; and if some of the commentary seems to break new ground then it is as well to remember that argument is worth starting as well as ending.

I am, as usual, indebted to a great many people for their help — to the authors and collectors of previous works (who have shortened procedure) and above all to Andrew Whyte of Jaguar Cars who not only opened doors but a great many dusty files and cupboards as well. The National Motor Museum at Beaulieu was its ever helpful self in the persons of Michael Ware and Eric Bellamy, and the many motoring magazines have yielded up their treasures. Lastly I am indebted to Lawrie Dalton himself, as much enthusiast as publisher, whose energy and help have made the exploration of every avenue a new pleasure.

Contents

FRONTISPIECE		3
AUTHOR'S NOTE		7
Chapter ONE	SIR WILLIAM LYONS	11
Chapter TWO	THE SWALLOW BODIES	17
Chapter THREE	SS	27
Chapter FOUR	SS JAGUAR	45
Chapter FIVE	JAGUAR and MARK V	61
Chapter SIX	THE XK SERIES	71
Chapter SEVEN	MARK VII, VIII and IX	97
Chapter EIGHT	2.4, MkII, 240 and 340	105
Chapter NINE	MARK X, 420G, S-TYPE and 420	111
Chapter TEN	E-TYPE	123
Chapter ELEVEN	XJ6 and XJ12	137
Chapter TWELVE	COMPETITION	149
Chapter THIRTEEN	ACQUISITION	179
Chapter FOURTEEN	PERSONALITIES and PERMUTATIONS	193

CHAPTER ONE

Sir William Lyons
Captain of, and Royal Designer for, Industry.

Few men have had so profound an effect on the world's motor industry as Sir William Lyons, and fewer still have left their own personal mark so clearly embedded in their products. On the one hand there have been the Bugattis, the Birkgits and the Bentleys of this world — great designers who have made great cars but were hardly captains of industry. On the other hand are the Sloanes, the Stokeses, and the Agnellis who have made and led vast industrial combines; but would probably be pushed to design a workable rice pudding. William Morris and Walter P. Chrysler came somewhere near bridging the gap; but William Lyons alone completely filled it.

From the first Austin Swallow to the latest XJ12 his cars have been HIS cars. Whether you like them or not they do not suffer from Dromedary's disease — a Dromedary being a Camel designed by a committee — and they are all so clearly the product of the same mind. They have led fashion rather than submit to it, and yet Lyons has been at all times sensitive to fashion in a marketing sense. His cars have always been what he thought the market wanted; and he has nearly always been right.

Of his business acumen there can be no doubt, and of it no questions are asked. As a captain of Industry he clearly earned his rank; and though board rooms may be private, balance sheets are not, so that at least once a year all is made clear to those who seek clarity. In another field, however, the plot thickens. There is an almost charming reticence at "The Jaguar" on the subject of William Lyons Royal Designer for Industry — and he himself has never spoken much of it. That he is proud of the distinction, and proud of his cars there can be little doubt; but beyond that kind acknowledgment he is as mum as "Brer Rabbit".

William Lyons as a young man on the Harley Davidson he raced at Blackpool Sands.

Sir William Lyons

A few discreet questions soon reveal that there are no drawings — either his or anyone else's — though, of course, final working drawings do exist, they come after the creation and not before or during it. It finally emerges that the only comparison to be made is to compare Lyons with the conductor of an orchestra who plays no instrument, makes no sound, and yet is fully and finally responsible for that performance of the Beethoven that you and the critics decide to love or hate. And just as good conductors at the end of the performance step down from the podium to take their bow with their musicians — so does Sir William, which is probably why he does not want to talk alone about being a designer.

His actual method has always been to work with one or two selected panel beaters, who had an uncanny sympathy with what the Maestro was after. A long collaboration of bits and pieces and models usually ensued, ending in a full scale mock up IN METAL. This was usually assembled in Sir William's front drive because he always wanted to see it in the daylight, in open air and in the kind of surroundings in which it would be finally judged. At this point it becomes a question of "no, that's much too long" or "we ought to push it up a bit here"—"that ought to come further back" "We'll have to do something about that window" and so on *ad infinitum,* until one sunny summer

With the then new SS100, left to right – E.H. Jacob, E.W. "Bill" Rankin (later Jaguar's Advertising Manager), The Hon. Brian Lewis (shaking hands with Lyons,) and Tommy Wisdom.

Sir William and a youthful Moss at the Daily Express Silverstone Meeting in 1952.

morning or biting February day according to the luck of the draw a mock up appears in the drive which is finally acceptable. Then the drawings are made and production of prototypes begins. There will be further detail modifications as there always are, but William Lyons R.D.I. has created another car.

    Having said that much all is plain sailing until you want to consider the kind of car he has created. There have been some unkind things said about some of them by some people; and if you raise the question at "The Jaguar" you will likely as not be greeted with groans of "Oh surely all that's over now"— well, of course it is — it's dead; but it won't lie down, and it is not likely to until somebody carries out an autopsy to try and make public the nature of the disease. This seems as good a chance as any.

    Lyons was always acutely conscious of his market — he would have achieved no comparable success if he had not been. The first Swallow saloons set out to offer on inexpensive chassis the kind of body that could only, up to that time, be expected on a much more expensive car. The Vee windscreens and overhanging peaks, the two-tone paintwork were all the things of the moment; and when he set out to make his first SS he was as much aware of the fashion as the next man. The *ne plus ultra* of those days was probably a Delage or an SSK Mercedes; both frequently to be seen with helmet wings and a small coupe on the short Chassis. He did not copy the cars but he did follow the fashion changes quickly and the long flared wings of the later models merely kept them up to date. True they were not very quick — not perhaps as quick as they looked; but they were not very expensive either and there was the rub.

Sir William Lyons

At that time the ordinary man in the street, and what is much more important the average Joan Hunter Dunn in the tennis club, was not nearly so well informed on the subject of motor cars as they are today; and one can well imagine the chagrin of the Merc owner who, hoping to get the girl to Budleigh Salterton for the week-end, was faced with the fact that not knowing an SSI from an SSK she went off to Brighton with some other chap. So hate is born — but the SSI was not vulgar though it may have been owned by some vulgar people. So were a number of Phantom IIs.

Surrounded by family and friends (with a youthful Lofty England on the extreme left) Sir William waits for his 1953 winner to cross the line at Le Mans.

Amid his fellow directors Sir William accepts one of the many tributes which crowned his last years as Chairman.

 Then came a sudden change. Rolls-Royce produced their first Bentley and set a new fashion for the "in" car. Wisely William Lyon followed suit — any fool would have done the same and he was certainly no fool. But by this time he had performance to offer as well; so some of the comment was still and an SS Jaguar merely became very good value for money — the marque was becoming established and had earned its good name. All seemed to be set for a rosy future — the plague had passed.

 After the war however a new plague was to come their way. The victories at Le Mans and the establishment of the Jaguar in its own right brought a new sort of jealousy. It was the car to have — the budding young executive could flash around the golf clubs and country clubs in a 3.8 quicker than was good either for his soul or the safety of the public. Awash with gin and tonic, as often as not like his car on the expense account, he was not the most likeable of people, and again an ill wind blew — not this time from the people who could well afford a fleet of Jaguars, but from people who could not afford them at all. To make matters worse those executive horrors, like other hunting beasts, tended to live in packs; and their mock Georgian sectors of near suburbia were quickly named "the Jag Belt"— but it was a passing phase. Furthermore it's an ill wind that blows no one any good, and many say that there is no such thing as bad publicity. At all events few cars have had a section of society named after them, and it was not long before the quality of the car itself redressed any ill feeling that might have been hanging about.

 In the end flattery healed the wound — for foreign importers, trying to cash in on the exclusive market Jaguar had built for themselves, upped the price of their imported models by anything up to a thousand pounds in order to steal the Jaguar market — and only succeeded, in the main, in stealing the opprobrium! Sir William and his colleagues were probably human enough to take some pleasure in the thought that he who laughs last laughs longest.

 Today Jaguar is assured of its position as one of the finest cars in the world, quite regardless of price; and if on the way to his goal, so surely reached before his retirement, Sir William occasionally found the going rough, it is unlikely that as a Captain of, and Royal Designer for, Industry he minded very much.

A seventieth birthday picture of Sir William and Lady Lyons in their home near Leamington Spa.

CHAPTER TWO

The Swallow Bodies

The first Austin Swallow left the Blackpool works in May 1927, just about five years after Lyons and Walmsley joined forces to manufacture sidecars. Walmsley had in fact been making sidecars before the partnership was formed; but the company had thrived on Lyons' sense of style on the one hand, and his business and production acumen on the other. Indeed the whole Jaguar story is a tribute to Lyons flair in these two seeming opposite directions. He had quickly seen that the average "chair" was an unsightly appendage to any decent bike and he had set about making something much more pleasing. It followed therefore that when he saw the Austin Seven, with its practical but far from lovely body, he should feel that he could do a great deal better. He also believed that he could do so without charging a great deal more ... and this is exactly what he did.

The car was an open two seater with a rounded tail the shape of half an egg ... and as soon as it was complete he set off to London in it to find someone to sell it. He found Bert Henly who not only took the agency but ordered five hundred. The Swallow Coachbuilding Company was on its way. A move to Coventry followed and the little two seater was given a hard top as an optional extra, which must now be regarded as well in advance of its time. A saloon soon followed and the style was set. For a brief period in 1927 the Company produced an open two seater on the Morris Cowley chassis but the advent of the M.Gs made its continued production somewhat superfluous. Saloons were introduced in 1930 on the Standard Nine, the Swift Ten and the 509A Fiat. They were of almost exactly similar design and unless the radiator was in view one would have been hard pressed to say which was which. After the Standard Company revised their front-end, it was hard to tell even head on which was Swift and which Standard. The Austin went on from strength to strength with its own Swallow radiator; but this too was given a centre strip to bring it in line. Nearly all the cars were finished in two tone paintwork either Green or Red covering the top half and wings while the side panels were in cream. A number of cars were all Cream in colour with only the wings and waistline in the contrasting tone — some were even black.

The interiors were well trimmed with heavy embossed leather and there was a general air of luxury. Vee windscreens were the order of the day with a big overhanging peak. Ventilators of nautical inspiration, graced the rear end of the scuttle (painted red inside) and a Swallow mascot was available. All this for little more than the cost of the standard product, so it is little wonder that the firm succeeded.

By 1931 the six cylinder Standard "Ensign" was joined to the fleet; and although not outwardly very different had, of course, much greater performance. It had an even greater significance since it was to lead a year or so later to the establishment by William Lyons of a new make of car. Before this happened however — or to be more exact while it was happening — the last flight of the Swallow was taking shape in the Wolseley Hornet. Lyons started offering an open two seater and a four seater on this chassis — the two seater being one of his happiest inventions with its neat "pinched" tail. Obviously his effort inspired others including the Wolseley Company themselves for they then

The Swallow Bodies

introduced a "Special" chassis for coachbuilders, with a slightly higher performance and better instruments. Swallow built for this too and the cars can be distinguished by the front-end treatment — the "Special" has the factory made cross-bracing before the radiator holding large headlamps and a horn, while the ordinary car has the headlamps attached to the wings. The Special had a six inch matching rev counter and speedometer while the other could boast of little more than its Morris Minor derived instrument cluster. They went on in production until 1933, by which time the developing SS cars claimed the whole of Lyons' attention, and Swallow bodies on other chassis ceased to exist — though the sidecars continued as a separate entity.

Brief Specifications

Swallow Bodied Cars 1927-1933.

Austin 7	4 cylinder	747 cc	2 Seater with detachable Hard Top Saloon
Morris Cowley	4 cylinder	1550 cc	2 Seater
Fiat 509A	4 cylinder	990 cc	Saloon
Swift "10"	4 cylinder	1190 cc	Saloon
Standard '9'	4 cylinder	1287 cc	Saloon
'Big 9'	4 cylinder	1287 cc	Saloon
Ensign	6 cylinder	2054 cc	Saloon
Wolseley Hornet	6 cylinder	1271 cc	2 Seater 4 Seater Tourer
Wolseley Hornet Special	6 cylinder	1271 cc	2 Seater 4 Seater Tourer

The second factory, in Cocker Street Blackpool, 1926. Note the combination, left, nearly on the forecourt — the car behind does not have a Swallow body.

H. Reed with an unknown passenger but a well-known sidecar.

One of the early chairs showing the hexagonal shape that was itself a trendsetter. The bike is an early 'Brough Superior'.

The body shop after the move to Foleshill, Coventry. About 1929 and a variety of shapes already evident.

Above and Below: *The original Austin Swallow photographed in Folkestone at the time of its introduction. The "hard top" seen below was a standard extra many many years ahead of its time.* Left: *The body shop at Coventry with the first saloons coming through on the left.*

Above: *One of the Survivors. This 1930 model, property of Mr. Donald Doughty founder of the Austin Swallow Register, is a Mark I model (no strip down the radiator).*

Right: *The paint shop (1929) note the absence of masks for the employees.*

Below: *The little saloon which for all its short wheelbase managed to achieve a good line.*

The rarest bird of all, the Morris Swallow. Dropped no doubt because of the M.G. which it so closely resembled (who thought of the "pinched" tail first, one wonders) it too was offered with the hard top as Bert Henly's advertisement shows.

When you see a SWALLOW BODY you may look for SUPER SPEED

THERE is something more than a touch of the thoroughbred in the Swallow bodied car. Performance lives up to appearance; an inspection and trial will convince you. The Swallow Morris or Austin is literally A NEW MODEL giving big car comfort and elegance.

See them at Henlys to-day.

PRICES:	Swallow Austin	Swallow Morris
With cape hood only	£175	£220
With coupe saloon head only	£185	£230
With cape hood and interchangeable coupe saloon head	£190	£235

HENLYS

SOLE SWALLOW DISTRIBUTORS FOR SOUTHERN ENGLAND (except Kent)

DEVONSHIRE HOUSE, PICCADILLY. Phone: Grosvenor 2271. HENLY HOUSE, 385-7 EUSTON RD. N.W.1. Phones: Museum 7734/9. 91, 155-157, GT. PORTLAND ST., W.1. Phones: Museum 7734/9.

1, 3 & 5, Peter Street, Manchester - Phone: Central 1780
Service Station: Hawley Crescent, Camden Town, N.W.1. Phone: Hampstead 5177

The Dark Corners of Olympia! Most interest attaches to the Standard on the right which has the old style radiator. Nearly all Standard Swallows were later and had a radiator in general shape much more like the Swift on the left. In the background the 509-A Fiat another rare bird.

If ever the magic words "the same only different" meant anything this was probably the moment. Above: The Standard 9. Centre: The Fiat 509A. Below: The Swift 10.

The famous Wolseley Hornet. Above: The two seater outside the Gretna Green marriage room is the standard car, while that in the centre is the special (the instruments are just visible). This view of the tail shows it to be surely one of Sir William's happiest inventions. Below: The 4 seater again on the ordinary chassis (as evidenced by the motor-meter and single wing — the special had a swan-like mascot).

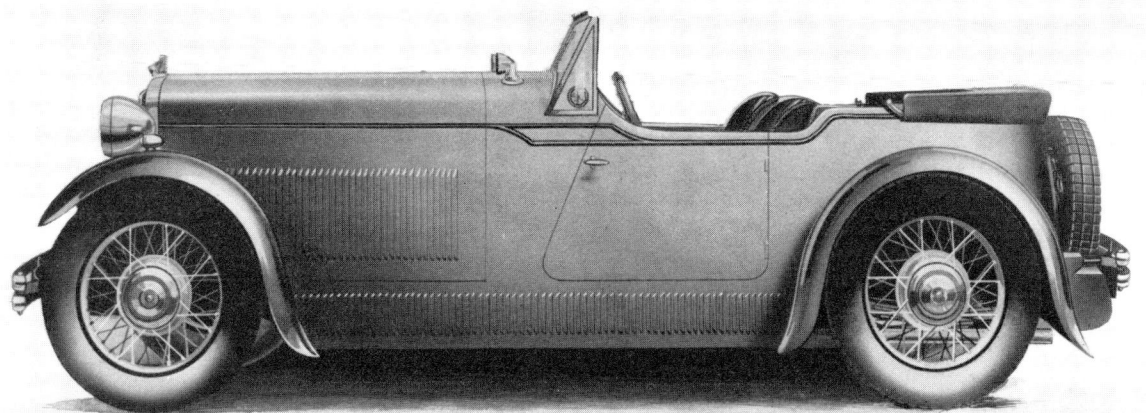

Olympia 1931. The introduction of the SSI and SSII (seen further over), while the Wolseley Hornet and Austin 7 are still going strong.

CHAPTER THREE

SS

By 1929 the Swallow Coachbuilding Company was producing something like a hundred cars a week and Lyons was looking round for new fields to conquer. Good as the existing cars were their design was largely dictated by the chassis on which the body had to be built, and he started to look for some way out of the dilemma. In 1930 the Company designed a chassis frame that would accommodate the Standard 16 and 20 h.p. engines, suspension and transmission units; and having got Rubery Owen to make it Lyons persuaded R. W. Maudsley, then Chairman and Managing Director of Standards, to supply his Company with complete chassis using this special frame. Seeking a name for the new product, "SS" was agreed between Lyons and Maudsley after long discussion, and not a little heat; it never being resolved whether the initials stood for Standard Swallow or Swallow Special.

The car was introduced at the 1931 Olympia show — and cannot be better described than it was in banner headlines in the Daily Express "The car with the £1,000 look for £310". It was introduced at a moment when fashion was on the change, for within a year its helmet type front wings and its somewhat claustrophobic interior were getting out of date and, after an interim design in 1933, Lyons came up for the 1933 Motor Show with the genuinely beautiful 1934 models with a much improved radiator and a "saloon" in which the rear passengers could look at the passing scene. The Coupé remained and a Tourer was added in early 1934. An Airline Saloon was announced at the 1934 Motor Show and a drophead Coupé joined the list in March 1935. The Airline was something of a compromise, the idea of a "streamline" back suddenly becoming very popular. Georges Roesch had started the rot with his Talbots, the Rover Company had had a go, and no lesser firm than Henri Labourdette had produced something very similar at the Paris Show on a Delahaye chassis. They all had one thing in common; and on the debit side — the back and the back wings were "streamlined" enough, but the front wings were the mixture as before, and in the case of the SS twin sidemounts didn't help.

Running parallel with all these cars were the SSII models — scaled down versions using the Standard 10 or 12 engine — very pretty little cars they were but naturally overshadowed by the bigger models.

Their place in society has been considered elsewhere in this book and need not be raised again. They did in fact go quite well by the standards of their day — they were smart and good looking and were well enough made. No better valedictory comment can be made than to quote Sir William himself: "The car, unfortunately, did not quite live up to the promise of its appearance for by no means could the engine be described as a good performer for its capacity". All the same it had done reasonably well in the Alpine Trial, had twice won the Concours de Confort in the unlimited Open Cars class in the "Monte" and had picked up no less than seven first class awards in the 1936 RAC rally. Not bad for a Cad's car.

Brief Specifications

SS Cars

1932

SSI — Engine 6 cylinder Standard 2054 cc (2552 cc optional extra) side-valve. Chassis and running units also provided by Standard Motor Co. 4 speed gearbox. Wheelbase 9' 4" Track 4' 1".

SSII — Engine 4 cylinder Standard 1052 cc side-valve. Chassis and running units also provided by Standard Motor Co. 3 speed gearbox. Wheelbase 7' 5½" Track 3' 9"

1933 Revision

SSI — Swept wings. Engines either 2054 cc or 2552 cc. Wheelbase 9' 11" Track 4' 3".

SSII — As 1932 but 4 speed gearbox.

1934 Revision

SSI — As 1933 but engine sizes increased to 2143 cc and 2663 cc and track increased to 4' 5".

SSII — Swept wings. Engine size increased to 1343 cc with the option of a 1608 cc engine. Chassis dimensions increased to: Wheelbase 8' 8" Track 3' 10½".

1935

SS90 — 6 cylinder Standard engine 2663 cc. Wheelbase 8' 8" Track 4' 6".

The original SSI with 16 hp Standard engine (the 20 hp was an optional extra) displaying all the "in" things of its day — long bonnet — helmet wings — hood irons and big headlamps with a tie-bar. An elegant car by any standards but despite the existence of a back seat, really a two-seater.

Two more views of the same car. From the front showing the original radiator — good enough at the time but soon due for change. The marked "tumble home" along the waist-line and the curious top hinges to the doors to make entry possible if not convenient for those about to be packed into the back. The side view gives a good idea of the long low image so desired at the time when power was related to bonnet length.

Cut-away drawings which reveal much of the original Standard from which the car was made. The sun-ray panels on the doors will also be seen in coloured glass on suburban houses and on the frets of early Pye radios. The bench-type front seat seems curious and the sliding roof reduced claustrophobia to bearable proportions.

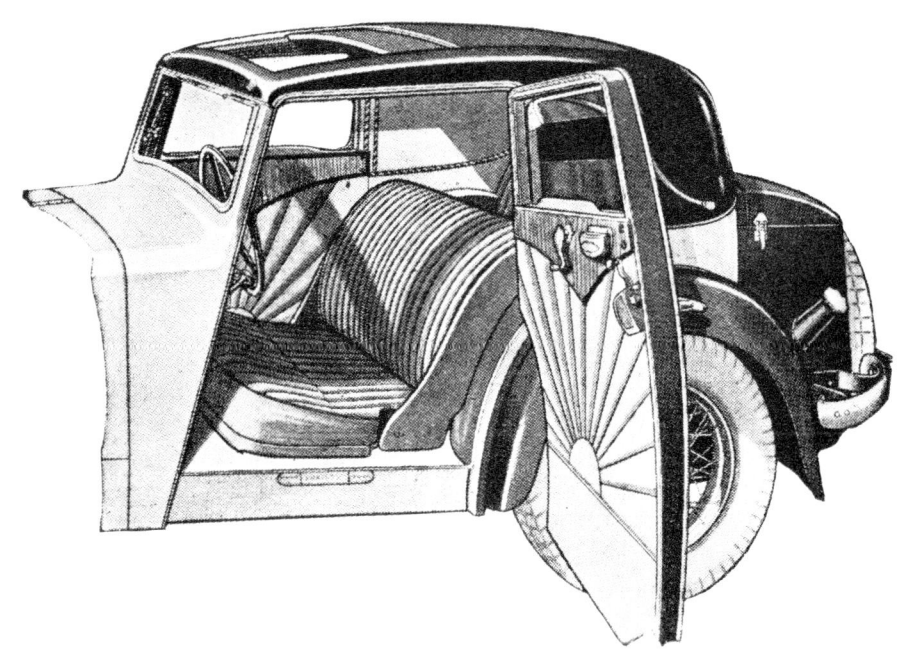

The first revision. Radiator unchanged but the tie-bar goes. The long wings were a demand of fashion, the longer body probably a demand of the customers — anyway it was now a four-seater. All else remained much as before and a little less good looking on the road than it was in the showroom.

The second revision, a new and much smarter radiator, and also light and a view for the rear passengers. The hexagonal SS motif appeared on the radiator and was repeated on the dashboard to repel the M.G. octagon. The airline saloon in the background of the top picture was a later addition (see page 36).

Another magnificent S.S.

THE NEW S.S.I. OPEN 4 SEATER

With the acknowledged return to favour of the open sports car the S.S. once again proves its leadership with this new open four seater model. Just as the S.S.I. saloon has swept the country, soon this long, low, sleek, open sports S.S. will be conspicuous on the roads everywhere.

Everything that the sports car enthusiast can wish for, this new S.S.I. model has—the same striking performance, the same striking beauty of line as the famous saloon, deep armchair seats providing perfect accommodation and comfort for four adults, 'closed-car' weather protection. Many striking colour schemes.

See it at Henlys *to-day*, so that you can be assured of early delivery. Full exchange and other facilities —of course.

Price (16 h.p.) **£325**. With 20 h.p. engine, **£335**.

The rear view—Low build, neatness of hood and instrument facia panel, large instruments dials . . . Driving visibility unusually good.

Interior view emphasizes the remarkable degree of comfort provided. Seating arrangement as the S.S.I. saloon. Real leather upholstery.

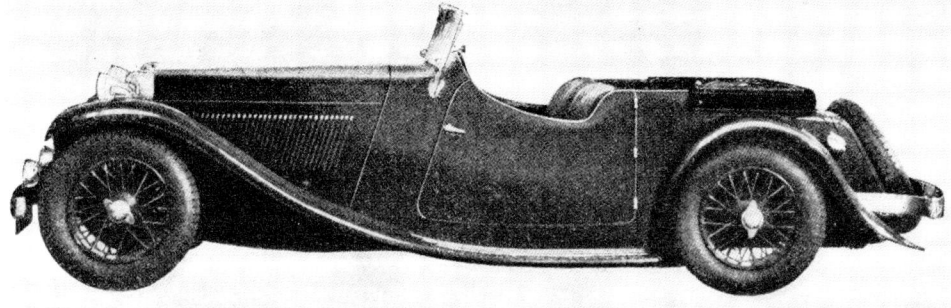

HENLYS

S.S. Distributors for Southern England.
Henly House, Euston Road, N.W.1.   Museum 7734 (20 lines).
Devonshire House, Piccadilly, W.1.
Heston Air Park (Aviation Dept.) Heston, Mdx.
MANUFACTURERS : THE SWALLOW COACHBUILDING CO. LTD., COVENTRY

The introduction of the tourer — a better word perhaps than sports car, pictures reveal the armchair back seats which were in the saloons as well and got over the problem of the lump for the differential so common in those days when rear passengers sat over the back axle.

For all the snide remarks the car did well in competition. Here is Needham at Shelsley.

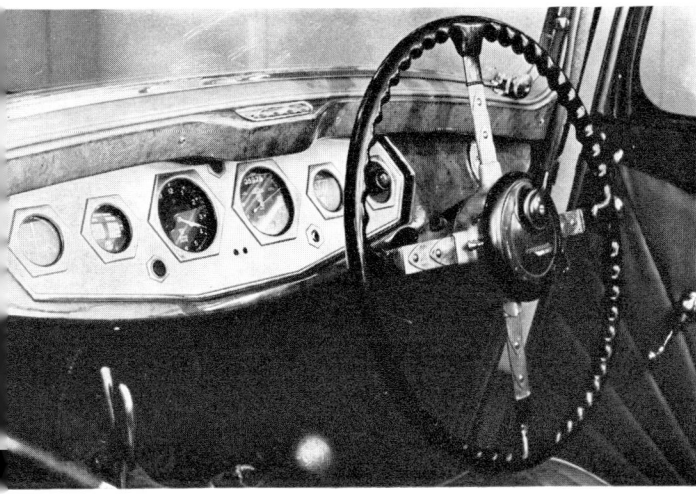

The famous hexagonal instruments of the SSI together with the laminated spring steering wheel much beloved on the continent at that time and therefore fashionable.

A second modification SSI now preserved in Holland. The hood and side screens do not look original, but in fact are — in design anyway.

Left: *The Airline saloon was an immediate success as evidenced by this winner of a continental concours. It seems a little comical now that having got wire wheels one covered them with "Ace" discs.*

Below: *Despite the fact that the back clearly did not know what the front looked like the Airline was much in fashion. Twin side-mounts were very snob and the smoother louvres in the bonnet helped. The built in "trafficators" behind the door is another sign of the times.*

The SS Blackpool Rally — a one make function. Here is J. L. Mason at the start of the elimination contest in one of the then new Airlines — note the chromium plated wheel rims — an SS feature.

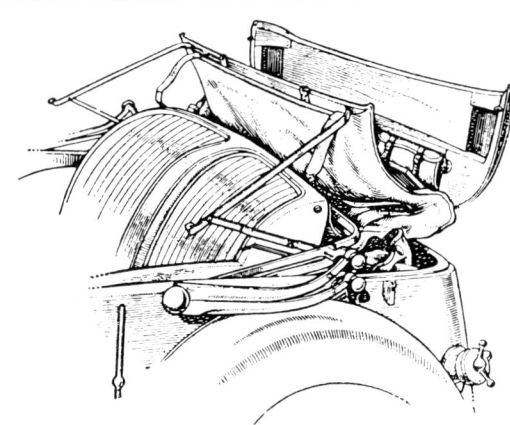

The rare-bird. One of the most handsome cars Lyons ever made with an exceptionally neat and clever hood storage (even if it did reduce the luggage space). Below: A. G. Douglas Clease who won a first class award in the 1935 RAC Rally.

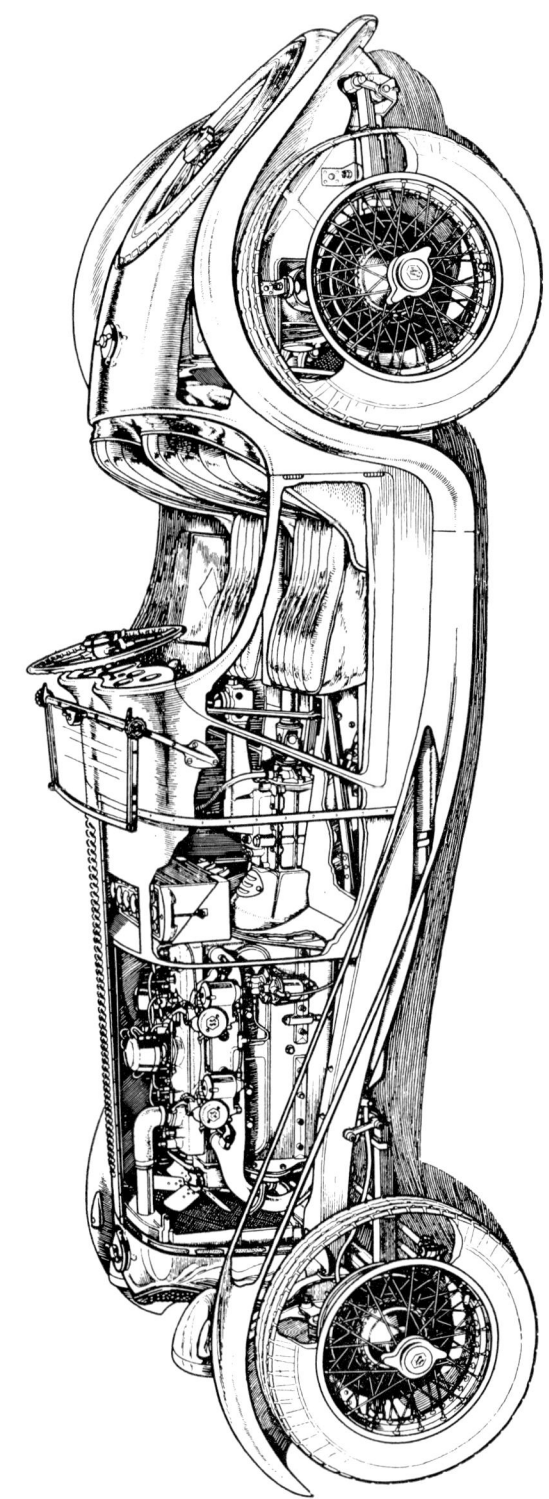

The original SS90 with side-valve Standard 20 engine and rounded tail, at this stage very much a new shape using the existing components. It was much changed before it ever got on to the market and up-rated to the SS100 very soon after.

The prototype SS90 (as opposite) with The Hon. Brian Lewis (now Lord Essendon) at the wheel. Lyons himself in one of the 23 SS90 built in 1935. The cars had the modified slab tank back seen below — a fashion presumably dictated by M.G. and Singer after Bentley.

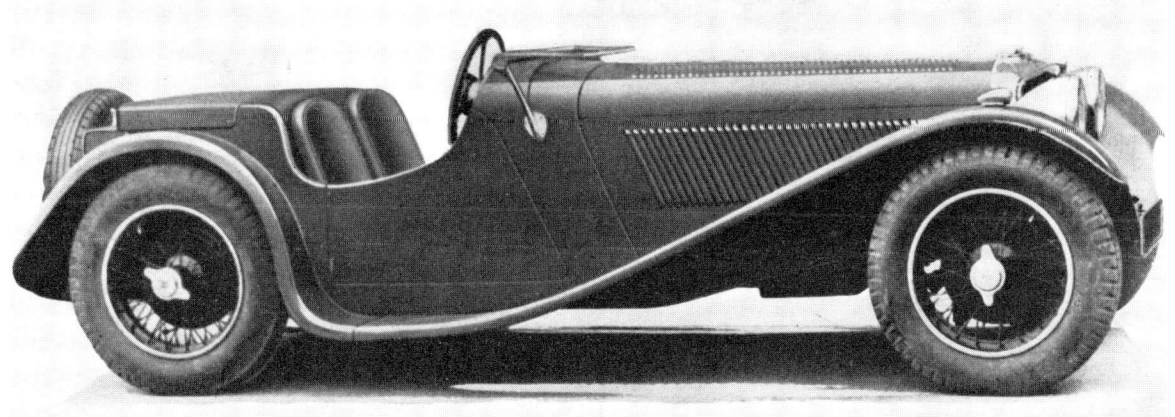

The original SSII design was not particularly happy, lacking the length of bonnet which saved its big brother. The revision was much more successful — but not in fact as long as this cut away drawing manages to suggest, as can be seen from the much re-touched picture opposite.

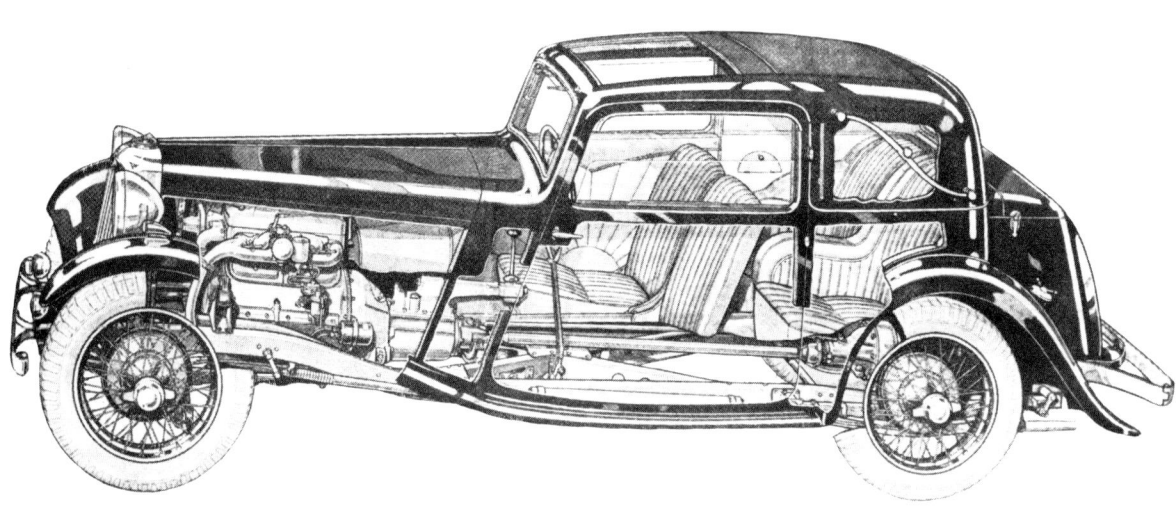

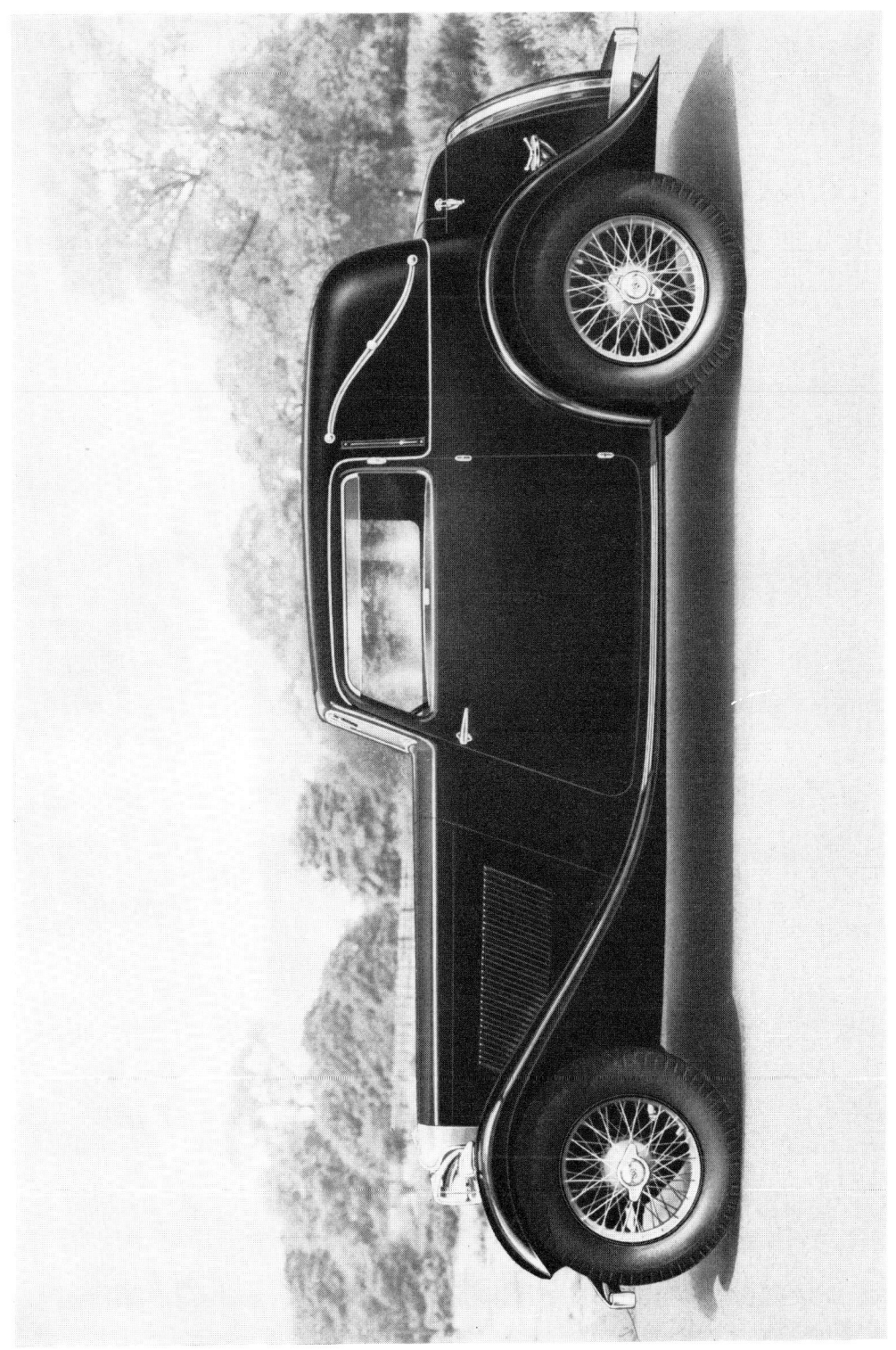

Fashionable people and competition success are among the mainstay of Motor Marketing and SS cars were as keen as most. Above: In *1935* R. E. S. Wyatt the Warwickshire and England Cricket Captain takes delivery of his SSII, while in the other two shots Mrs J. M. Piggins does well in Class C in the Blackpool Rally.

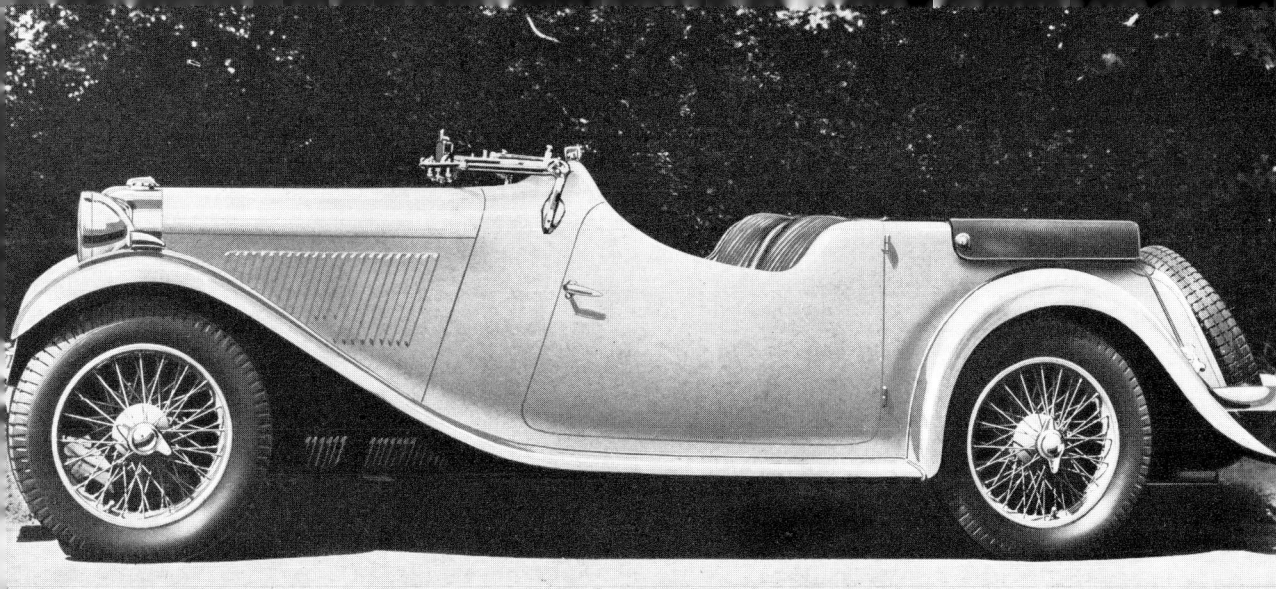

The SSII really came off best in its open form (even with the hood up!) and showing the flag was all part of the competition programme.

The strength of the SS Club is well shown by these pictures of Rallies at Buxton and Blackpool. Careful observation, particularly of the lower picture, shows clearly the different effects of colour often making similar models look either longer or taller.

CHAPTER FOUR

SS Jaguar

The car was announced at the May Fair Hotel where the assembled dealers were asked to guess the price. An average of their guesses was made, which, according to Sir William, came to £765. There was some delighted consternation therefore when it was announced that the selling price would actually be £395.

The new car with its 2½-litre engine, attractive price, and a top speed of some 90 mph (from 104 bhp) was an immediate success, its four doors making it much more generally acceptable than the previous models had been. In parallel of course were the new 1½-litre models (actually 1608 cc) using more or less unaltered Standard engines.

The next big change came in 1938 with the introduction of the all steel models with a slightly more bulky but generally better appearance (the spare wheel went into the boot) and in addition a drop-head coupe of very elegant design. This had in fact been foreshadowed by a Swiss coachbuilder (p 58). A revised 1½-litre on similar lines now had an o.h.v. engine and to crown it all a 3½-litre model was made available, which really did have some go.

This interest in performance was all part of a well organised plan and as early as 1935 the company had produced and marketed in small numbers the SS 90 using the 20 hp side valve engine in a short chassis. It was fitted with a body of the then popular "Le Mans" shape; but with long flared wings of great beauty, almost as if a blending had been made of the best of an MG midget with the Barker Continental Phantom II! It went quite well but as soon as the o.h.v. 2½ and 3½-litre engines became available it was re-named the SS Jaguar 100 (though it was almost always referred to simply as the SS 100) and really started a competition career — particularly in the hands of Tom and Elsie Wisdom and the Hon. Brian Lewis. It was the first change that Lyons so much wanted to see; the move away from appearance as an end in itself towards appearance coupled with genuine performance. The fact that the 2-litre independently sprung 328 BMW was about its equal in performance worried no-one: for SS cars the tide had turned, and they were about to take it on the flood.

Brief Specifications

SS Jaguar

1936

2½ litre — 6 cylinder ohv engine (push rod) built by Standard Motor Co. to design by William Heynes based on a modified Standard side-valve unit 2663 cc. Chassis and running units also supplied to special design mostly by Standard Motor Co. Body with wood frame. Wheelbase 9′ 11″ Track 4′ 6″.

1½ litre — 1608 cc Standard side-valve engine. Wheelbase 9′ 0″ Track 4′ 0″.

1938 Revision

3½ litre — Engine as 1936 but 3485 cc.

2½ litre — Engine as 1936. Body on steel frame re-designed radiator, spare wheel mounting, and other details. Wheelbase 10′ 0″ Track 4′ 8″.

1½ litre — Engine modified to ohv and capacity increased to 1776 cc. Body and details as larger cars. Wheelbase 9′ 4½″ Track 4′ 6″.

SS100 — Engine either 2½ or 3½ litre. Wheelbase 8′ 8″ Track 4′ 6″.

The arrival of the Jaguar brought with it the Bentley look and the end of the long low line. These three are all 2½-litre models.
Top: *Mathews in the Welsh Rally.*
Centre: *Price in a Jaguar Club event — the two-tone paint is non-standard.*
Bottom: *R. E. S. Wyatt the Warwickshire Cricket Captain (centre) with S. H. Newsome on his left.*

The "old" open body was retained for a year or two and used with the new O.H.V. engine. Points of identification are the new radiator (same as the saloons) and the larger brake drums.

As with the previous range a "baby" was included. No longer called the SSII but known as the 1½-litre Jaguar it followed as closely as possible the shape of its larger brother. A shorter bonnet and front wings pushing the side mount up above the body line is a give away (shared with the 1½-litre M.G.!)

Above: *Song and Dance Man Bobby Howes in the film "Sweet Devil" in which two cars of the same model were used.*

The most famous of the pre-war models — and perhaps the most elegant car Lyons ever made — the SS Jaguar 100. Grown from the SS 90 seed (see page 39) it had real performance. It was in great demand by both sportsmen and the nobility — Prince Michael of Rumania (below).

The sportsmen included Tommy Wisdom (seen here at Bo'ness) Mrs. I. McLennan (in a Club Rally) and E. H. Jacob who won the last individual award and helped SS cars to the team prize in the 1937 Welsh Rally.

The cars were revised for the 1937 Show with all-steel bodies. The side-mounts disappeared. The side moulding was modified and its radiator and wings changed slightly. As before 1½-litre, 2½-litre and 3½-litre saloons were offered — absolutely fashionable in their day — a Bentley for less than half price! Left and Above: *3½-litre cars.* Below: *A 1½-litre car.* Next Page: *The interior was really very smart and properly luxurious. Separate knobs for each windscreen wiper which had to be "parked" by hand to get it out of the way of the opening screen operated by the cranked lever at the top of the dash.*

An interesting look into the future. The SS Jaguar 100 coupé which never went into production (1938) and the XK120 which did — no mistaking the mind behind either of these two.

The drop head coupé was the most handsome — no mere convertible could hope to match it. The dark car spoiled by the war time headlamps but wearing fashionable 'Ace' discs shows the effect of a light hood on a dark car and also the satisfactory compromise between shape when up and compactness when down.

Special bodies began to appear, there being always someone who thinks he can gild the lily. Above: By Maltby was at least different and could be had on 1½- and 3½-litre chassis. Inside it had hand painted hunting scenes covered by glass plate on the garnish rail. Centre: This one said to be by Magill & Co. of Sheffield looks so absolutely standard that we can only think the caption to be a terminological inexactitude. Below: By Tuscher of Zurich which must have looked beastly with the hood folded in the German manner.

Above: *S. H. Newsome had this coupe built on the 100 chassis, reminiscent of the Atalanta it might well have had commercial possibilities.* Below: *Captain Black of Standards had this "limousine" built by Mulliners of Birmingham for his wife. The razor-edge style had become the sine qua non for coachbuilt Bentleys so why not follow suit? "Limousine" presumably referred to the fact that it had a division.*

The SS Jaguar stand in 1938 — notice the prominence of the word Jaguar — can we ever again really believe that the decision to call the cars Jaguars was entirely post war. 'The Autocar' referred to the red coupé in the words of a then popular song, "the little red caboose behind the train".

CHAPTER FIVE

Jaguar and Mark V

The flood tide which had been felt so strongly at the SS works in the late 'thirties unhappily led not in the direction of commercial expansion but in the direction of a world war; and it was not until this was nearly over that Sir William Lyons plans for future development could once more be given full consideration.

It's an ill wind that blows no-one any good and out of the horrors of 1939-45 came some solid gains for the company in terms of factories and equipment. Some months before the end of the war the company were given the "go-ahead" to consider their post war production. As a first consideration they had to do something about their name, since the initials "SS" had grown more than a little tarnished with the passage of hostilities. As they were already using Jaguar as a model name for their whole range it was a logical step to use it generally for the company in the future; and having cleared the situation with Armstrong Siddeley (who had used the name for an aero engine) SS Cars disappeared and Jaguar Cars became the order of the day.

As with every other manufacturer all they could hope to do in the first instance was to carry on where they had left off — and for some people such a proceeding was not all that difficult; but for Jaguar there were real problems. The Standard company, who had hitherto made the engines, were totally committed to their new Vanguard model; and Black their Managing Director told Lyons that he would be unable to continue production. He did however offer to sell the necessary plant. Within days Lyons had sent transport for the plant and a cheque to pay for it, so that when Black had second thoughts, and suggested that they revert to the old arrangement, Lyons replied "No thank you, John, I have now got the ball and I would rather kick it myself!"

As soon as production of the pre-war cars had got under way, plans for the future needed to be hurried forward. However, since these were on a massive scale, involving a quite new engine, some kind of interim car was needed to bridge the gap — and the answer was the Mark V. Interim solutions are seldom the best and the Mark V was certainly not the best Jaguar — but it was good enough. It used a body shell not unrelated to the previous models with a curved rear quarter light that was to be a feature for many years to come. Cable brakes gave way to hydraulics, the headlamps were faired in, as was the fashion of the day; and a box section frame with independent front suspension much improved the ride even if it did little for the road-holding. By the standards of its day it was a smart car — if you like, something of a step back in the Jaguar plan, being a bit of a Cad's car — but great men have often taken a step back before leaping forward; and as that leap was planned for October 1948 the step back was well worth while.

Brief Specifications

Date	Model	No. of Cylinders and Engine Dimensions	Gearbox and Ratios	Suspension	Brakes	Wheelbase and Track	Price from
1946	Jaguar 1½ litre	4 73 × 106 mm 1,776 cc 65 bhp @ 4,500 rpm	4-speed, synchro. 4.87, 7.08, 11.84, 19.21:1	Semi elliptic front and rear	Girling rod-operated	9 ft 4 in 4 ft 4 in	1946: £684 1947: £787 1948: £865
	Jaguar 2½ litre	6 73 × 106 mm 2,663 cc 102 bhp @ 4,600 rpm	4-speed, synchro. 4.55, 6.12, 8.82, 15.36:1	Semi elliptic front and rear	Girling rod-operated	10 ft 0 in 4 ft 6 in	1946: £889 1947: £991 1948: £1,089
	Jaguar 3½ litre	6 82 × 110 mm 3,485 cc 125 bhp @ 4,250 rpm	4-speed, synchro. 4.27, 5.74, 8.28, 14.41:1	Semi elliptic front and rear	Girling rod-operated	10 ft 0 in 4 ft 6 in	1946: £991 1947: £1,099 1948: £1,199
1949	Mk. V 2½ litre	6 73 × 106 mm 2,663 cc 102 bhp @ 4,600 rpm	4-speed, synchro, 4.55, 6.21 9.01, 15.35:1	Independent front, semi elliptic rear	Girling 2LS hydraulic	10 ft 0 in 4 ft 9½ in	1949: £1,189 1950: £1,247
	Mk. V 3½ litre	6 82 × 110 mm 3,485 cc 125 bhp @ 4,250 rpm	4-speed, synchro. 4.3, 5.87, 8.52, 14.5:1	Independent front, semi elliptic rear	Girling 2LS hydraulic	10 ft 0 in 4 ft 9½ in	£1,263

Above: *Immediately after the war everyone went back to making the 1939 models. Here are $1\frac{1}{2}$-litre models coming off the line — the only change being the absence of "SS".*

Below: *Exports were the order of the day and the wire wheels were still covered by 'Ace' discs. $3\frac{1}{2}$ litres awaiting delivery.*

Above: A magnifying glass is the only way of telling which side of the war this photograph is dated — but the Jaguar sticker on the screen helps. Centre: A "convertible" in New York where it was an immediate success. Below: the curves on the hood were not quite as smooth as the advertisements make out — but it was a handsome car.

The Specialists were at it again. Above: *At a Belgian Concours d'Elegance in 1948, first prize went to this 3½-litre with coachwork by Van den Plas — behind it a pre-war SS100 rebodied by the same coachbuilder and shown at the Brussels Show the same year.*
Below: *A 3½-litre coachbuilt by the Swiss coachbuilder Langenthal with front end entirely reminiscent of the current Alfa Romeo 2500.*

The Mark V was an interim model — but the first new Jaguar after the war. Above: *One of Sir William's famous mock-ups and* Below: *the car as it actually appeared.*

Not the best looking Jaguar but a handsome car by the standards of its day — with traditional British interior which no doubt helped its American Sales.

More to set the social scene than explain the car — film fans are invited to do their own guessing.

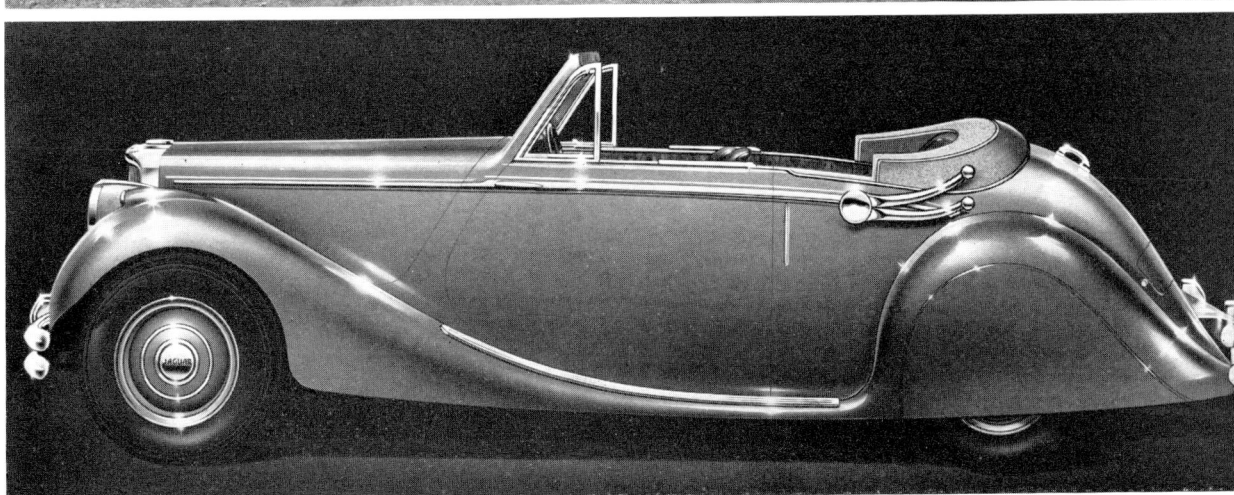

Always a firm favourite until present safety regulations ruled it out — the drop-head with 3-position hood looked very good indeed . . .

... even when seen in Chicago overlaid with extras and leading the American Legion Parade with Generals Ferry and Gates and the Lt. Governor of Illinois driven by owner Mr. D. C. Cooper.

CHAPTER SIX

The XK series

The introduction at the 1948 Motor Show of the XK 120 sports car in general, and the XK engine in particular, was the turning point in Jaguar history — the moment that William Lyons had long waited for and carefully planned. If up to that time his cars had been good lookers first and performers afterwards they now had both in full measure. Just as they had on several previous occasions, the Press lost their hearts (and quite a few of them their heads) to the new model. It was an instant, raving success.

Lyons' talent as a designer of bodies was recognised in 1956 when he was appointed a Royal Designer for Industry; but no amount of talent in that direction would have taken his company to the heights it reached in that decade without his astonishing business flair; and, to be fair, the work of William Heynes and his team in producing the XK engine.

The first 120 open two seater was quickly followed by a Coupe of great beauty (shades of Jean Bugatti's "Atlantique") and a drop head and powered by the new engine they had the market by the horns — cars costing two or three times as much did not look half so good.

The new twin overhead camshaft unit was not only to power five Le Mans winners; but also a whole range of both large and small saloons, and still to be a remarkable power unit some twenty-five years later. It is a heavy thing with a lot of cast iron in it which makes it retain its heat; but it is very reliable and in the "D" type versions produced well over 250 bhp. When all is said and done in the history of motoring there have been few engines to hold a candle to it.

In what seemed to be no time the XKC, now almost universally known simply as the "C" type, was introduced — the "C" standing for competition — and of its feats we shall tell elsewhere, only the long nosed model made for Le Mans in 1952 suffered any setback at all; and, vexing as that must have been, it was not anything of great import.

1955 saw the XK 140 with a little more room and in the eyes of many, now that the cars are becoming collectors pieces, the finest of them all. With it came the "D-type" and the full flowering of the Jaguar competition effort — one could call it the last of the great racing sports cars, for after its demise the whole style and shape of sports car racing changed. The point is perhaps best made by Jaguar themselves who produced in very small numbers the XKSS which was in fact nothing but an everyday road version of the D-type.

After all this the XK 150 was, understandably perhaps, something of an anticlimax. A fine car, but the svelte looks of its predecessors had been lost. It was more roomy, more sensible and in some ways even a better car; but it did not make the heart beat faster as the other two had. The time was ripe for something quite new which, needless to say, Sir William Lyons had up his sleeve.

Brief Specifications

Date	Model	No. of Cylinders and Engine Dimensions	Gearbox and Ratios	Suspension	Brakes	Wheelbase and Track	Price from
1949	XK120	6 83 × 106 mm 3,442 cc 160 bhp @ 5,000 rpm	4-speed, synchro. 3.64, 4.98, 7.22, 12.29:1	Independent front, semi elliptic rear	Lockheed 2LS hydraulic	8 ft 6 in 4 ft 3 in	1950-1: £1,263 1952: £1,678 1953: £1,759 1954: £1,601
1951	C-type	6 83 × 106 mm 3,442 cc 200 bhp @ 5,800 rpm	4-speed, synchro. 3.31, 3.99, 5.78, 9.86:1	Independent front and rear	Lockheed 2LS hydraulic	8 ft 0 in 4 ft 3 in	£2,327
1955	XK140	6 83 × 106 mm 3,442 cc 190 bhp @ 5,600 rpm	4-speed, synchro. 3.54, 4.28, 6.2, 10.55:1	Independent front, semi elliptic rear	Lockheed 2LS hydraulic	8 ft 6 in 4 ft 3½ in	1955: £1,598 1956-7: £1,692
	D-type	6 83 × 106 mm 3,442 cc 250 bhp @ 6,000 rpm	4-speed, synchro. 3.54, 4.52, 5.82, 7.61:1	Independent front and rear	Dunlop disc	7 ft 6 in 4 ft 2 in	£3,878
1957	XKSS	6 83 × 106 mm 3,442 cc 250 bhp @ 6,000 rpm	4-speed, synchro. 3.5, 4.5, 5.8, 7.6:1	Independent front, semi elliptic rear	Dunlop d.sc	7 ft 6 in 4 ft 2 in	Approx. £3,750 if sold in U.K.
	XK150	6 83 × 106 mm 3,442 cc 190 bhp @ 5,500 rpm	4-speed, synchro. 3.54, 4.54, 6.58, 11.95:1	Independent front, semi elliptic rear	Lockheed 2LS hydraulic	8 ft 6 in 4 ft 3½ in	1958-9: £1,763 1960: £1,666
1958	XK150S	6 83 × 106 mm 3,442 cc 250 bhp @ 5,500 rpm	4-speed, synchro. with overdrive 3.18, 4.09, 5.247, 7.60, 13.81:1	Independent front, semi elliptic rear	Dunlop servo-assisted d.sc	8 ft 6 in 4 ft 3½ in	£2,065

Above: The introduction of the XK120 was a true highlight in Jaguar history. This is the original mock-up prototype then known as the XK100/120. As it might at that time also have appeared in 4-cylinder form.
With little changed save the shape of the screen, the car swept all before it — art and engineering have seldom been so well blended.

Light colours seemed to suit it best — and this early model displays the separate side lamps.

Left: *The cockpit displays a neat blend of contemporary sports and Jaguar traditional.*

Below: *Export drained the home market to make the desirable almost unobtainable.*

A later dark car — sidelamps now part of the wing moulding.

The drop head coupe — by popular demand — sacrificed some of the good looks for a kind of convenience demanded by the British climate.
One the other hand the fixed head coupe had the same kind of Bugatti charm that was seen in the one-off SS100 before the war. This must surely be a collectors piece of the future.

Above: *The famous were proud to be among the known owners. Here is Neville Duke — famous test pilot and world record holder. Spats had to go when wire wheels arrived because of the hub caps.*
Below: *The 1952 "Montlhéry" XK120 which averaged 100 mph for no less than a week at the famous French circuit.*

The Specialists were rarely as good as the originator and some of the efforts to gild the lily were almost too awful to contemplate. Above: A brave effort at an early hard-top by W. M. Park of Kew and an Abbott 4-seater, both had function rather than looks on their side.
Below: An early Pininfarina, very conscious of the current Ferrari/Maserati/Pegaso style.

Above: *Stablimenti Farina (the 'old' firm) at the 1952 Turin Show — called the Flying Jaguar. There was a drop head too known as the Golden Arrow (See pp 104)* Centre: *This rather bulky convertible was by Beutler with brass-headed upholstery tacks on door trim and fascia.*
Below: *Carrosserie Oblin of Brussels — more in the Ferrari tradition than ever; but it made second place in the 1951 Liege-Rome.*

After the excesses of his competitors it's nice to return to Lyons. Above: the XK140 roadster looking as sleek as ever. Below: The 140 coupé shows how the line had to be spoiled to make space. As for the rear wheel spats — you either like them or you don't.

Above: *The heavy bumpers front and rear were the main difference in profile between the 140 roadster and the 120.*
Below: *A coupé without the spat and in a darker colour — looks much sleeker than the one opposite.*

Above: *The rather wider strips in the grille were fashionable rather than better and matched the Mark II's vee screen. May seem dated but it was good looking.*
Below: *The drop-head managed to keep most of the roadster dash — looked better with the hood up.*

The drop-head with hood folded — not every private owner achieved such a neat effect every time. The big jump behind the door opening is all that spoils an immaculate line.

A very "Jaguar" inside with dangling keys to scratch the veneer, a time controlled trafficator switch (top centre) but the potentially dangerous bulge in the centre of the steering wheel had gone.

Ghia (Turin) on the XK140 at the height of his American involvement. Overtones of the Chrysler Specials with a very Facel Vega windscreen.

Above: *Ghia (Aigle) on the XK140*. A little happier than the Italian car. This was exhibited at the Geneva Show in 1956 some six months after the one opposite appeared at Turin.
Below: ODD but distinctive — and typical of its creator, Raymond Loewy the cultivated American Industrial Designer. It was built by Boano in 1955.

The 150 chassis which gives a good idea of its strength and balance.

The 150 followed on the pattern set out by its predecessors. Some of the slender charm was lost in making it more spacious and it was less of a sports car. To say it was clumsy would be going too far, but line for line it was no match for the 140. In almost all other aspects it was better; but it did not handle as well.

Best of the bunch was the open two seater now called a "roadster"— and as all the pictures on this page show cars with left hand drive then no-one will be surprised.

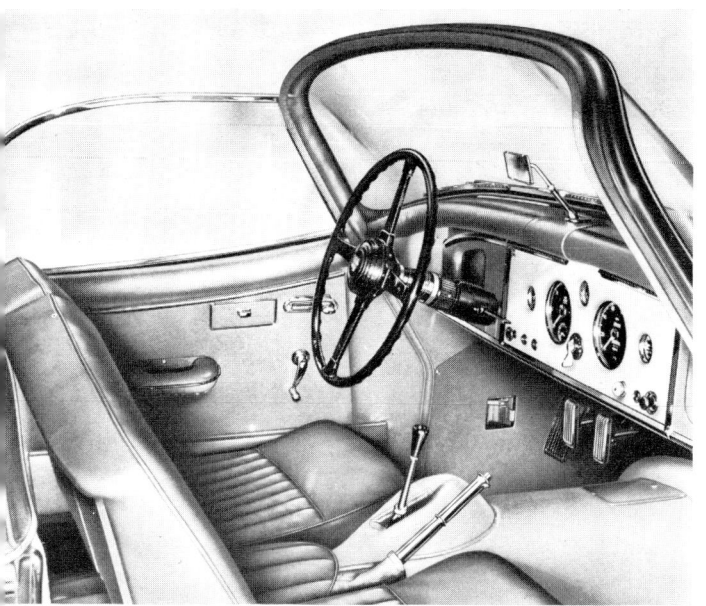

Inside it was goodbye to the walnut dashboard — and it was goodbye to the vee screen as well. Some special models were built and could be distinguished by the small "S" on the door as shown below.

Above: *One of the few special bodies to be seen in the U.K. This by Bertone is certainly one of the happiest. Little Jaguar touches being retained in the bumpers and radiator grille.*
Left: *No collection of photographs is complete without the mystery picture. This one claims to be the interior of a special bodied Jaguar but by whom or where is not vouchsafed.*

This rather beautiful body by Michelotti is built on a D-type chassis which must make it one of the most desirable cars ever.

The Prototype 'C' — C standing simply for Competition as applied to the original XK. The centre picture gives a good idea of its construction.

While the other two besides giving an idea of what the car looked like also remind us of how crude the facilities were at racing circuits in those days!

Here one of the most famous C-types the 1951 Le Mans winner is seen on the way to the race from the works. Below: One of the few Jaguar disasters the 1952 "droop snoot" Le Mans model. The idea was better airflow, but in the event this proved so good that not enough went in through the grille to cool the engine.

The interim "C/D" development car, which first appeared in late 1953 — it had yet to grow its tail.

One of the most famous of all sports racing cars — the Jaguar D type. Seen here in its two principle guises. Above: *The original "short nose".* Below: *The later and tidier "long nose".*

The XKSS — rare bird indeed. In fact a road going version of the D-type, few were made and several destroyed in the great factory fire of 1957. By the time everyone had recovered the E-type was on its way so no more were made.

CHAPTER SEVEN

Mark VII, VIII and IX

Against the slim splendours of the sports cars, Jaguar now felt the need to move in a slightly new direction — into the plain luxury market. Up to the Mark V the saloons had been what we were then pleased to call "Sports Saloons"; but just as Bentley, following of course its more exclusive brother, had moved more into the world of open luxury, so did Jaguar.

Nowadays the Mark VII does not look all that good, from a long term classic point of view it was one of Lyons' less successful efforts; but it is easy to criticise with the benefit of hindsight. At the time it was announced it looked fine, and with all the power of the XK engine under its bonnet, it was indeed a magnificent car. The subsequent Mark VIII and IX, although altered and improved in detail, were as near as dammit the same car. The need to slim down the looks brought the introduction of a chromium beading and two colour trim — a trick that had been successful on the prosaic Austin and Morris saloons not long before and now worked well enough on more distinguished panels.

The car became exclusive, frequently chauffeur driven, boasted picnic tables once more and, as an optional extra, even a division. It was in a way something of a boat of a car, known, no doubt with envy, in certain circles of Bristol as the "Jews Canoe" it nevertheless showed up well in the Monte Carlo Rally where a degree of responsive handling is an absolute essential!

Leaving all else to one side it followed one aspect of the Jaguar tradition in a most unmistakable way — and that was in terms of value for money. Introduced in 1951 at £1,276 as the Mark VII and bowing out as the Mark IX ten years later at £1,884 it had all its possible competitors laid flat. Add to that its most remarkable component the XK engine and it was little wonder that the rest of Europe's motor industry went round scratching its head wondering how it could be done for the money.

Brief Specifications

Date	Model	No. of Cylinders and Engine Dimensions	Gearbox and Ratio	Suspension	Brakes	Wheelbase and Track	Price from
1951	Mk. VII	6 83 × 106 mm 3,442 cc 160 bhp @ 5,000 rpm	4-speed, synchro. 4.27, 5.84, 8.56, 14.4:1	Independent front, semi elliptic rear	Girling 2LS hydraulic with servo assistance	10 ft 0 in 4 ft 9½ in	1951: £1,276 1952: £1,694 1953: £1,775 1954: £1,616
1955	Mk. VIIM	6 83 × 106 mm 3,442 cc 190 bhp @ 5,600 rpm	4-speed, synchro. 4.27, 5.17, 7.44, 12.73:1	Independent front, semi elliptic rear	Girling 2LS hydraulic with servo assistance	10 ft 0 in 4 ft 10 in	1955: £1,616 1956: £1,711
1957	Mk VIII	6 83 × 106 mm 3,442 cc 210 bhp @ 5,500 rpm	4-speed, synchro. 4.27, 5.16, 7.47, 12.73:1	Independent front, semi elliptic rear	Girling 2LS hydraulic, servo-sasisted	10 ft 0 in 4 ft 10 in	£1,830
1959	Mk IX	6 87 × 106 mm 3,781 cc 220 bhp @ 5,500 rpm	4-speed, synchro. 4.27, 5.48, 7.94, 14.42:1	Independent front, semi elliptic rear	Dunlop servo-assisted disc	10 ft 0 in 4 ft 10 in	1959: £1,994 1960: £1,884

Note: Automatic gearboxes were first fitted to the Mark VIII and to all subsequent Jaguar models as an optional extra.

Three stages in the creation of the Mark VII, originally with Bentley type front wings and in the centre an interesting slope to the centre pillar. Finally the car more or less as the production model.

The Mark VII full of current Jaguar touches in side-lights and bumpers and in a dashboard clearly derived from the Mark V. The big knob in the centre of the steering wheel was still in evidence.

Above: *A convertible by Beutler (1953) — very Swiss and all but indistinguishable from countless others.*

Below: *Almost unbelievable vulgarity from no less a person than Pininfarina — but it won a Grand Prix d'honneurs at Cannes Concours d'Elegance for its owners Mr. & Mrs. Embiricos — of pre-war Bentley fame.*
(The lower photograph is almost certainly Monte Carlo, as are the registration plates.)

Two-tone colour schemes took some of the lumpiness out of the then slightly ageing shape and a curved windscreen helped the Mark VIII to keep up with the times. The inside was plush — to quote Jaguar at the time — "the richly appointed interior (is) carried out in figured Circassian walnut".

The steering boss is now flat and the overdrive switch can be seen on the screen rail just by the vertical spoke of the wheel. The shape was at its best in light colours. Jaguar caption reads "Mark VIII or IX" their guess must be as good as any!

These two cars, one hard one soft top, were produced on the Mark VII chassis by Stabilimenti Farina (the old firm) for a Belgian distributor. They carry the names Golden Arrow for the drop-head and Meteor for the coupé and are relatives of the car on pp. 79. Least said soonest mended.

CHAPTER EIGHT

2.4, Mark II, 240 and 340

While the Mark V had moved away from the compact sports saloon, this was naturally a market that Jaguars were very loath to give up; and it is not surprising, therefore, to find that with the demise of the Mark V and the introduction of the larger car in 1951 it was only a question of time before a new smaller Jaguar appeared. This was the 2.4 introduced in 1956. This was the first effort to reduce the 6 cylinder XK engine to a smaller capacity, and one of the great benefits was the reduction in the quantity of cast iron, and with it the chance to improve weight distribution (especially on a smaller car).

Even as originally conceived it was a nice tubby little car, compact and swift and an excellent addition to the range from a marketing point of view. A 3.4 version was soon added and in 1957 a much improved Mark II version was introduced. Here Lyons reverted to the rear window treatment he had used on the Mark V and later the Mark VII — the car looked lighter and an opportunity was taken to modify several dimensions and generally improve its road holding which on the original had not been up to what had by then become Jaguar standards.

The new Mark II was also offered in 3.8-litre form principally one supposes for the American Market; but it quickly made a name for itself in a series of more or less demonstration "Saloon Car" races organised at the principal meetings in Great Britain — and later went on to achieve similar fame throughout the world. It really was quite a package; and became a new kind of Cads Car for a new kind of Cad — although by that time he would probably rather have been referred to as a Senior Executive!

These models were among the most successful cars to emerge from the works — they were driven and loved by many different sorts of person and generally carried the Jaguar image to wider fields. With the Le Mans victories behind them no-one could question their engineering and they were right in so many ways that their universal appeal is not surprising. It was into this body shell that the V8 Daimler engine was also successfully introduced — but of that, more elsewhere.

Towards the end of their successful run the 3.8-litre was dropped and the other two models became known as the 240 and 340 — but the only noticeable difference was a new narrow bumper the original Jaguar "twin" was beginning to look a little outmoded. Automatic transmission was available as on the big cars.

Brief Specifications

Date	Model	No. of Cylinders and Engine Dimensions	Gearbox and Ratios	Suspension	Brakes	Wheelbase and Track	Price from
1956	2.4 litre	6 83 × 76.5 mm 2,483 cc 112 bhp @ 5,750 rpm	4-speed, synchro. 4.55, 6.21, 9.01, 15.35:1	Independent front, semi elliptic rear	Lockheed Brakemaster 2LS servo-assisted hydraulic	8 ft 11 3/8 in 4 ft 6 5/8 in	1956: £1,344 1957: £1,430 1958-9: £1,495 1960: £1,445
1957	3.4 litre	6 83 × 106 mm 3,442 cc 210 bhp @ 5,500 rpm	4-speed, synchro. 3.54, 4.54, 6.58, 11.95:1	Independent front, semi elliptic rear	Lockheed Brakemaster 2LS servo-assisted	8 ft 11 3/8 in 4 ft 6 5/8 in	1957-9: £1,672 1960: £1,579
1960	2.4 litre Mk II	6 83 × 76 mm 2,483 cc 120 bhp @ 5,750 rpm	4-speed, synchro. 4.27, 5.48, 7.94, 14.42:1	Independent front, semi elliptic rear	Dunlop servo-assisted disc	8 ft 11 3/8 in 4 ft 7 in	£1,534
1960	3.4 litre Mk II	6 83 × 106 mm 3,442 cc 210 bhp @ 5,500 rpm	4-speed, synchro. 3.45, 4.54, 6.58, 11.95:1	Independent front, semi elliptic rear	Dunlop servo-assisted disc	8 ft 11 3/8 in 4 ft 7 in	£1,66.
	3.8 litre Mk II	6 87 × 106 mm 3,781 cc 220 bhp @ 5,500 rpm	4-speed, synchro. 3.54, 4.54, 6.58, 11.95:1	Independent front, semi elliptic rear	Dunlop servo-assisted disc	8 ft 11 3/8 in 4 ft 7 in	£1,779

The prototype 2.4 — the beginning of a new breed of Jaguars. Rather "quieter" in concept than the final car, it was very much in keeping with its times.
The 2.4 as it first appeared with several Jaguar signatures added — most of them chromium plated.

Again the original 2.4 — at its best in light colours.
Later versions had modified rear wheel spats which lightened the car a good deal.
A 3.4 version was soon introduced and with wire wheels looked better still.

The Mark II version was a different dog beneath the skin with a wide track among other things. The car was made lighter to look at and more pleasant for rear passengers by changes to the rear quarter and rear window. The new rear window shows well in this picture taken, for publicity purposes no doubt, in Russia. The rear spats have been removed which helped tyre changes if not the appearance.

Later models had the fog and spot lamps set in where the ventilation grilles had been (compare with top picture). A 3.8 model was also introduced.

Towards the end of the run the 3.8 was dropped and the other cars designated 240 and 340. The bumpers were re-designed, the spotlights dropped (so the grilles came back) and the steering wheel made more slender (as on the S-type), otherwise as the picture shows it was the mixture as before.

CHAPTER NINE

Mark X, 420G, S-type and 420

Here seems to be for the first time a recognition, in marketing terms, that Jaguar was growing — a development of models rather than startling new departures — all of them better than their predecessors, all anticipated, and all living up to the public expectation.

Firstly the Mark X. Clearly the Mark IX had had its day, and the big new car was both better looking and much better engineered — its independent rear-end giving it a magnificent ride and excellent road manners. It started life with the 3.8 engine in 1962 and was given the 4.2 unit in '66 — the price was now over £2,000 which put it "up market" and made it one for the Chairman — who would admit to being no kind of Cad at all. Quite why it had in the end to be called the 420G is not very obvious — save that it was part of a process of change that can be more clearly traced in the smaller cars.

The S-type was a logical development of the Mark II — indeed its body shell was a clear derivative. Like the Mark X it was given independent rear suspension which much improved its roadability; and if its new shape was not quite so "all of a piece" as some of its predecessors, then it at least followed the lines of the bigger cars to make a kind of family feeling.

In 1967 the Company came as near as it has ever done to doing a "face-lift"— a device well known throughout the world's motor industry but one not hitherto countenanced by this Company. The 420 was in fact an S-type with a new front, in line with that on the old Mark X, now called the 420G. With these cars came a new Daimler Sovereign which was simply a 420 with a different radiator and minor changes of trim within. The engine had by now lost its polished aluminium rocker covers and boasted a black box with polished "fins" on top bearing whichever name was appropriate to the radiator. *Sic transit gloria mundi*.

It is not to suggest for one moment that the cars lacked anything a prospective purchaser might have deemed himself entitled to if he bought a "Jag" (a word which had by now worked its way into Common English Usage); but the Company were once more at the gestation stage and new cars of this ilk do not appear overnight, the gestation period being more Elephantine than Human — and there were, as there always are at the "Jaguar" other things on the way.

Brief Specifications

Date	Model	No. of Cylinders and Engine Dimensions	Gearbox and Ratios	Suspension	Brakes	Wheelbase and Track	Price from
1962	Mk X	6 87 × 106 mm 3,781 cc 265 bhp @ 5,500 rpm	4-speed, synchro. 3.54, 4.54, 6.58, 11.95:1	Independent	Dunlop servo-assisted disc	10 ft 0 in 4 ft 10 in	£2,392
1964	S-type 3.4 litre	6 83 × 106 mm 3,442 cc 210 bhp @ 5,500 rpm	4-speed, synchro. 3.54, 4.54, 6.58, 11.95:1	Independent	Dunlop servo-assisted disc	8 ft 11½ in 4 ft 8¾ in	£1,669
	S-type 3.8 litre	6 87 × 106 mm 3,781 cc 220 bhp @ 5,500 rpm	4-speed, synchro. 3.54, 4.54, 6.58, 11.95:1	Independent	Dunlop servo-assisted disc	8 ft 11½ in 4 ft 8¾ in	£1,758
1965	Mk X 4.2 litre	6 92.1 × 106 mm 4,235 cc 265 bhp @ 5,400 rpm	4-speed, synchro. 3.54, 4.7, 6.98, 10.76:1	Independent	Dunlop servo-assisted disc	10 ft 0 in 4 ft 10¾ in	£2,156
1967	420G	6 92.1 × 106 mm 4,235 cc 245 bhp @ 5,500 rpm	4-speed, synchro. 3.54, 4.7, 6.98, 10.76:1	Independent	Dunlop servo-assisted disc	10 ft 0 in 4 ft 10 in	£2,238
	420	6 92.1 × 106 mm 4,235 cc 245 bhp @ 5,500 rpm	4-speed, synchro. 3.54, 4.7, 7.44, 10.76:1	Independent	Dunlop servo-assisted disc	8 ft 11⅜ in 4 ft 7¼ in	£1,930

The Mark X was a tremendous step forward both in engineering and in shape — few could deny that it was real competition for the Bentley of its day and it was certainly grand enough to stand without the Forth Bridge to prop it up.

The graceful tail encompassed an immense boot at the cost of prodigious overhang. The purposeful front heralded a new Jaguar radiator and incorporated both the grilles and the lamps which had been so ambivolent in the Mark II and as usual it looked its best in light colours — though less markedly than most.

The interior was in the best Jaguar tradition with walnut veneer, soft leather, picnic tables and heating to the rear compartment. The dash followed the lines of the Mark II including the long line of tumbler switches which seemed so excellent at the time and have been so denigrated ever since; but who wants ergonomics when they can have pleasure?

The S-type clearly derived from the Mark II and heralded the Mark X, and while both front and back were clearly extensions of an earlier model the mechanics were much improved. The new tail managed to do away with the infuriating spat, carried more luggage and encompassed two petrol tanks — one on each side — either or both of which emptied with alarming speed.

Inside it was the mixture as before, and whether wire wheels helped or hindered was a matter of personal taste. An interim car perhaps but a very successful one.

It took a clever chap armed with an up-to-date Glass's guide to tell a 420G from a Mark X but there were differences — a chromium strip down the side and some not too happy dual colour schemes.

The only noticeable diffence between these 420G pictures and the Mark X on page 115 is that this car has electrically operated windows; but that was also an optional extra on the previous car, as was the limousine division.

The 420 — really an S-type with a Mark X radiator began to make the family resemblance more complete. With less space to play with the grilles had to be squashed.

A very quick looking car, it heralded the XJ6 and in that respect if no other, a marvellous example of the continuous line of Sir William's mind. The clock in a thick roll of black padding went some way to please the anti-walnut group but Sir William wisely knew they didn't really count in his market.

A very beautiful body by Bertone on a 3.8-litre S-type but it looks much too like a German Motorway Coupé to have any real Jaguar feel about it. When all is said and done few coachbuilders ever did half as well as the canny old R.D.I. himself.

CHAPTER TEN

E-Type

With the huge success of the "D-type" in competition, the small flirting with the XKSS and the acknowledged triumph of the original XK 120 under their belt, it was necessary, one feels, to their salvation as well as to their markets, that the Company should once again produce if possible the ultimate in Sports Cars — and when the E-type was announced in 1961 it was clear that they had done just that.

Millions of words, almost entirely of praise have now been written about the E-Type; and there is little if anything to add. Either at its original price of only just over £2,000 or at its present price in 12-cylinder form of £3,319 it remains genuine competition for the European glamour cars costing anything up to four times as much. True, in England, it is now a common enough sight to lack the excitement of the Italian Masterpieces, and it has perhaps never had an entirely outstanding shape — nevertheless it is a Lyons creation in his best vein, and no doubt now that a new engine has been added a new body is not far off — one can only hope that Sir William planned it before his retirement, though we must one day face the fact that there is going to be a Jaguar that does not have those flowing lines which are so entirely individual to the one man.

It started life as a 3.8 but soon enough that model was dropped in favour of the 4.2., which can't have been that much better, but was that much more sought after. The open car is perhaps more handsome than the coupe — though offering even less baggage space than the closed model — though judging by its capacity to pick up a baggage when when necessary the average young man (and his baggage) can probably make do with a very little luggage. The latest factory hard top is a handsome addition.

Of course there was a cry for more seats and the 2+2 model was introduced. Not such a good looking car but obviously a more useful one. With the introduction of the V-12 engine there were small styling changes which have again improved its appearance. No longer the *dernier cri,* it is holding up well until the replacement arrives.

Derived from the D-Type it has itself enjoyed more than a little competition success, particularly in the hands of private owners — many of whom had produced special lightweight versions. It is today what the XK 120 was when it was introduced, and were it not for the fact that Lyons always could recapture his first fine careless rapture, one would say it was his ultimate achievement.

Brief Specifications

Date	Model	No. of Cylinders and Engine Dimensions	Gearbox and Ratios	Suspension	Brakes	Wheelbase and Track	Price from
1961	E-type	6 87 × 106 mm 3,781 cc 265 bhp @ 5,500 rpm	4-speed, synchro. 3.31, 4.25, 6.16, 11.18:1	Independent	Dunlop servo-assisted disc	8 ft 0 in 4 ft 2 in	£2,098
1965	E-type 4.2 litre	6 92.1 × 106 mm 4,235 cc 265 bhp @ 5,400 rpm	4-speed, synchro. 3.07, 3.9, 5.34, 8.23:1	Independent	Dunlop servo-assisted disc	8 ft 0 in 4 ft 2 in	£2,033
1966	E-type 4.2 litre '2+2'	6 92.1 × 106 mm 4,235 cc 265 bhp @ 5,400 rpm	4-speed, synchro. 3.07, 4.07, 6.06, 9.33:1	Independent	Dunlop servo-assisted disc	8 ft 9 in 4 ft 2 in	£2,245
1971	E-type (Series III)	12 90 × 70 mm 5,343 cc 254 bhp @ 6,000 rpm	4-speed (o/d optional)	Independent	Girling disc all round	8 ft 9 in 4 ft 6 in	£3,319

The prototype for the E Series on test in North Wales and clearly showing its D Type ancestry.
CUT 7. *A special racing lightweight E-type created for Dick Protheroe and now part of the Robert Damey collection.*

Surprisingly these are all pictures of the same car. E2A Top left it is seen at the April practice without it's tail. It was raced at Le Mans later that year, 1960, and is shown in other pictures in Briggs Cunningham's American Colours. It is very much half D and half E.

When it first appeared the E-type roadster had much the same impact as the original XK120. Despite the alternative of the coupé (opposite) a works "hard-top" was available.

Opinions are fairly sharply divided as to which car looked better. In terms of practicability as regards luggage if nothing else the closed car won hands down.

Over the years there were many minor modifications. Here is the 4.2 with "open" lamps — and the 2 \ 2 coupé with what the works call the steep screen.

Handsome enough from any angle — it's a funny thing that when wire wheels are the order of the day something more solid starts to look more attractive. These are the later models with open headlamps.

This is the Series Two car — impressive as ever from the front particularly without number plates while the interior is a fine blend of comfort and function. The switches, reminiscent of the Mark II are now of less penetrating design.

For comparison, above the 2+2, below the 2 seater and in the middle the +2 part. The top half of the seat squab folds to make a platform for luggage.

Princess Grace and, hidden by the windscreen highlights, Prince Rainier of Monaco in an E-type course car — a smiling Louis Chiron stands mid-bonnet. The other two cars are Series III one with works hard top.

Although originally to be available with either V12 or XK engine all Series III ended up as V12's. The seat of power became tidier and automatic was an alternative. Both shape and wheels are changed.

A special lightweight E-type owned by G. B. Corser — it bristles with "mods" and is one of the few still running with an aluminium block.

CHAPTER ELEVEN

XJ6 and XJ12

New Jaguars are apt to burst upon the world unannounced — at least they were in the good old days when new cars appeared at motor shows; but the arrival of the XJ 6 was eagerly awaited, for news of a fabulous new Jag was about some months before the car. The cynics were enjoying wondering if the old firm would keep pace with changing trends and maintain their position; but, as usual, when considering the brain children of Sir William Lyons the cassandras were disappointed.

At the time the XJ 6 was announced we were in a period of square cars; and square cars have never been part of Sir William Lyons imagination. He therefore became once more a trend-setter, for the XJ 6 was all Jaguar, all curves and yet so completely a car that no single voice could be raised in disapproval. It is true there was a little sadness about the radiator — the 420 and 420G design seeming to have so much to commend it; but it was only the loss of a friend, and the new shape soon became quite as apparently right as it had been to its creators.

As for the mechanics, the XK engine proved to be as good as ever, and a good deal better than many much younger designs, for it had been constantly and consistently developed. The suspension, both front and rear, embodied all the know-how that competition and West-End motoring had together taught the designers; and the car went like a bomb, handled like a dream, and within a month of its announcement could not be had for love nor money.

The 4.2-litre version made the strongest appeal to those who believe that there is no substitute for litres and a 2.8 version was appreciated in those parts of Europe where the tax man had the same idea.

That leaves only the 12 Cylinder car to be considered — and what is there to say. To make it at all was only to gild the lily, and yet there was every reason for doing so. The V-12 engine has always been the most glamorous type of unit in the world and, apart from the need for engineers to develop, there is the constant threat of new pollution laws with the possibility of reduced power from any given size of engine. Above all clearly the engineers wanted to make it and the public wanted to buy it, and no entrepreneur of Sir William's quality would want to stand in their way on the eve of his retirement!

As this book goes to press the new two-door models are announced — probably the best looking, best performing Jaguars that have ever been made; and with imagination one can see in them the dream of the young man who, some forty years ago, when he produced the first SSI, had dreamed of just such a car. It is not given to many of us to realise so much.

Brief Specifications

Date	Model	No. of Cylinders and Engine Dimensions	Gearbox	Suspension	Brakes	Wheelbase and Track	Price from
1969	XJ6	6 92 × 106 mm 4,235 cc 170 bhp @ 4,500 rpm	4-speed (o/d optional)	Independent	Girling disc all round	9 ft 1 in 4 ft 10 in	1969: £2,254
	XJ6	6 83 × 86 mm 2,792 cc 140 bhp @ 5,500 rpm	4-speed (o/d optional)	Independent	Girling disc all round	9 ft 1 in 4 ft 10 in	1969: £2,102
1972	XJ6L	6 92 × 106 mm 4,235 cc 170 bhp @ 4,500 rpm	4-speed + o/d	Independent	Girling disc all round	9 ft 5 in 4 ft 10 in	£3,415
	XJ12	12 90 × 70 mm 5,343 cc 254 bhp @ 6,000 rpm	3-speed (automatic only)	Independent	Girling disc all round	9 ft 1 in 4 ft 10 in	£3,672
	XJ12L	12 90 × 70 mm 5,343 cc 254 bhp @ 6,000 rpm	3-speed (automatic only)	Independent	Girling disc all round	9 ft 5 in 4 ft 10 in	£3,994
1973	XJ6 Series Two	6 92 × 106 mm 4,235 cc 170 bhp @ 4,500 rpm	4-speed (o/d optional)	Independent	Girling disc all round	9 ft 1 in 4 ft 10 in	
	XJ6L Series Two	6 92 × 106 mm 4,235 cc 170 bhp @ 4,500 rpm	4-speed + o/d	Independent	Girling disc all round	9 ft 5 in 4 ft 10 in	
	XJ6C Series Two	6 92 × 106 mm 4,235 cc 170 bhp @ 4,500 rpm	4-speed (o/d optional)	Independent	Girling disc all round	9 ft 1 in 4 ft 10 in	
	XJ12L Series Two	12 90 × 70 mm 5,343 cc 254 bhp @ 6,000 rpm	3-speed (automatic only)	Independent	Girling disc all round	9 ft 5 in 4 ft 10 in	
	XJ12C Series Two	12 90 × 70 mm 5,343 cc 254 bhp @ 6,000 rpm	3-speed (automatic only)	Independent	Girling disc all round	9 ft 1 in 4 ft 10 in	

Note: The XJ12 four door model on the normal wheelbase has been phased out. The 2.8 litre XJ6 in Series Two form is only available in certain continental markets.

Here is the XJ prototype in one of its earlier forms — clearly a two door design but incorporating many previously tried Jaguar design features against the grain are the twin headlamps and the angular roof line over the rear window.

Here it is again — this time outside Sir William's front door — the tail already beginning to look like the production car. The front we have been told posed many problems — this effort presumably being one of them. Below: A pre-production model "uglied-up" for road test purposes.

A one-off royal cabriolet. In these safety conscious days it would presumably not make a production model — pity. It was locally converted for a Royal Tour of Mauritius in 1972.

This is the standard XJ6 — the best car yet. Different in so many ways and yet unmistakably Jaguar.

and inside it is the same — and that row of switches mercifully remains — ergonomics be damned!

After all the talk the 12 cylinder finally appeared — in the same body shell. To some it seemed to be gilding the lily — but to others it was the ultimate Jaguar. At all events the engine was a new departure. Not the twin-cam twelve that appeared in the mid-engined sports prototype (page 202) but a single cam per block design. In the course of gestation nearly every great name in the game was involved. Heynes, Hassan, Mundy and Weslake for a start.

A long wheelbase car was a logical step. The one above is an XJ6 and below an XJ12, but details of trim apart they are the same. Centre: How the extra inches are used.

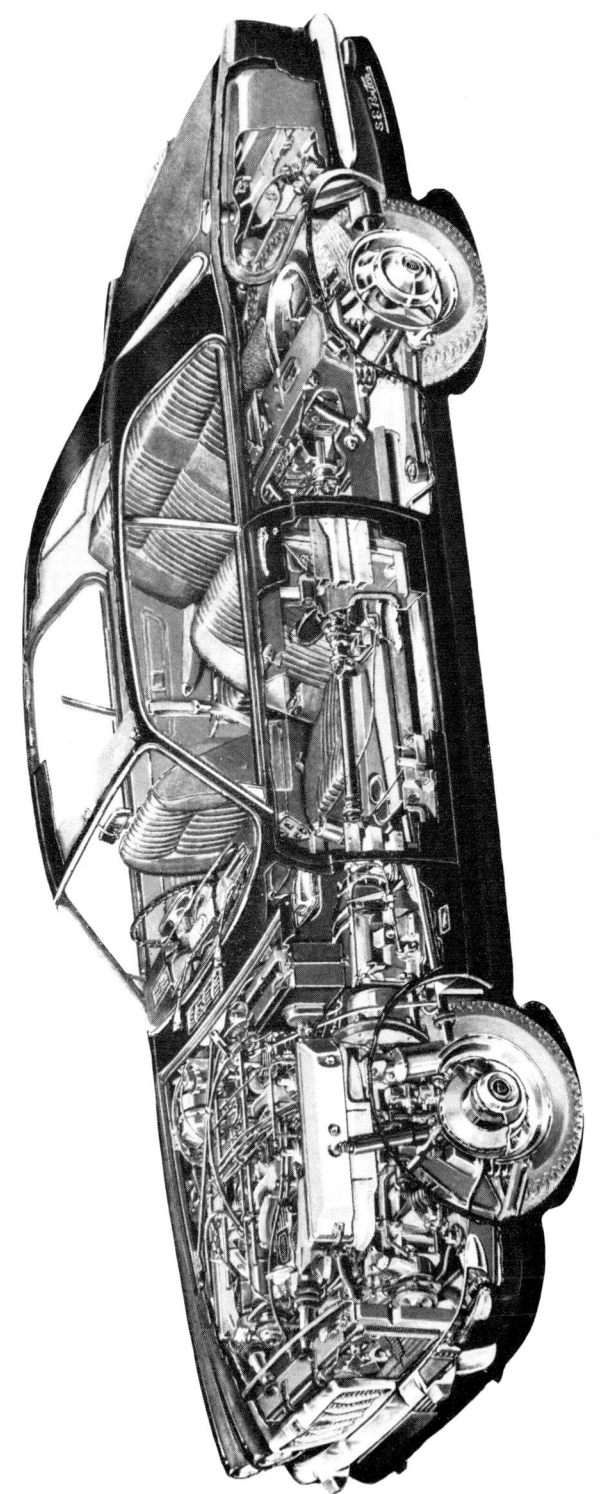

The new Series Two Jaguars announced in September 1973 included this two door body, illustrated here by S. E. Porter's beautifully executed cut-away drawing.
This is designated the Series Two XJ6C or XJ12C and as C cannot mean Competition in this context, it must surely mean Coupé.

Above and below. The XJ6C complete with vinyl covered roof and disappearing windows. Centre. The four door saloon with the new front common to all Series Two XJ6 and XJ12 Jaguars. Only the badge differentiates the six from the twelve.

CHAPTER TWELVE

Competition

The competition story begins very soon indeed after Lyons had established himself as a manufacturer, rather than a coachbuilder. The original Helmet-wing coupe offered little chance; but the following year when the first of the swept-wing tourers was in production both a works team and some private owners entered for the Alpine Trial. The works team met with little success, but the private entrants managed 6th and 8th places. Not world shattering perhaps, but in those days to finish an Alpine at all was a not inconsiderable achievement.

The first real success came with the introduction of the "SS 100" when Tommy Wisdom and his wife put up the best overall performance in the Alpine. The car was widely seen in many club events, did well in the RAC Rally and even after the war, when new sports cars were scarce, the 100s kept the flag flying in the early years. Only one "100" was actually built after the war, and with this Ian Appleyard won his first Coupe des Alpes, and the last big victory, before the XK 120 took over, was again Appleyard who took 2nd place in the 1949 Tulip.

As soon as the new car was introduced it enjoyed some competition success; and achieved a good deal more record breaking at Jabbeke. Johnson got a 5th in the Mille Miglia and Moss won the TT. Before saying goodbye to the XK 120 as a competition car one must record Appleyard's Alpine Gold Cup (the first ever awarded) for three successive Coupes des Alpes; and the Claes Ickx (father) victory in the Liege/Rome/Liege at the time the toughest of all "rallies"— and it was in fact much more of a race.

Then came the immortal "C" and "D" types and the five victories at Le Mans — equal to the Bentley record and putting Jaguar in a position no other manufacturer in the world could match. There were, too, a vast number of successes in other events some of major importance and some not — but while there were still genuine sports cars racing, the Jaguar remained untouchable.

In parallel to this the new 2.4 and subsequent Mark II saloons started off on a new career in saloon car races — if some of the early events at Silverstone were little more than demonstrations no-one enjoyed them any the less for that — and a later victory at the Nurburg Ring put paid to any idea that the car was not, in the right hands, fully competitive.

Now the racing is over — the firm has grown, the products have to some extent changed and, as with a number of European manufacturers who likewise have not been unsuccessful in competition, the firm does not need it any more. The present day promotion-orientated circus has little appeal to the kind of men who, in the fifties, paralleled the Bentley boys. The E-Types nowadays do well in what are basically club events, particularly in America, and the mid-engined twelve cylinder prototype shows that those in command at Sir William's factory have not lost sight of the possibilities.

Some notable SS and Jaguar Firsts

Date	Event and Class	Drivers	Model
1934	Monte Carlo Rally: *Concours de Confort* Unlimited Open Cars	S. H. Light	SSI
1935	Monte Carlo Rally: *Concours de Confort* Unlimited Open Cars	Hon. B. E. Lewis	SSI
1936	International Alpine Trial: Best individual performance irrespective of class	T. H. Wisdom Mrs. E. M. Wisdom	SS100 2½ litre
	Shelsley Walsh: 3,000 cc class	S. H. Newsome	SS 100 2½ litre
	Welsh Rally: Class One	E. Jacob/D. Hand	SS Jaguar 2½ litre
	Class Two	R. Sandford	SS Jaguar 1½ litre
1937	R.A.C. Rally: General Classification	J. Harrop	SS100 2½ litre
	Welsh Rally: Best overall performance	E. H. Jacob	SS100 2½ litre
	Brooklands: October Long Handicap	T. H. Wisdom	SS100 3½ litre
1938	Paris-Nice Trial: 3,000 cc class	T. H. Wisdom	SS100 2½ litre
	Monte Carlo Rally: *Concours de Confort*	J. Willing	SS Jaguar 3½ litre
1939	Shelsley Walsh: 5,000 cc class	S. H. Newsome	SS100 3½ litre
1948	International Alpine Rally: Over 3,000 cc class, *Coupe des Alpes*	E. I. Appleyard	SS100 3½ litre
1949	Production Car Race, Silverstone	L. G. Johnson	XK120
1950	Tourist Trophy, Dundrod	S. Moss	XK120
	International Alpine Rally: Best individual performance, *Coupe des Alpes*	E. I. Appleyard	XK120
1951	Rallye Soleil, France	H. Peignaux	XK120
	International Tulip Rally: Overall winner	E. I. Appleyard	XK120
	Production Car Race, Spa	J. Claes	XK120
	R.A.C. Rally: Open cars over 3,000 cc	E. I. Appleyard	XK120
	Le Mans 24-Hour Race	P. N. Whitehead P. D. C. Walker	C-type
	International Alpine Rally: Best individual performance, *Coupe des Alpes*	E. I. Appleyard	XK120
	Liege-Rome-Liege Rally: General Classification	J. Claes/J. Ickx	XK120
	Tourist Trophy, Dundrod	S. Moss	C-type
	Tour de France: Over 3,000 cc class	Hache/Crespin	XK120
1952	British Empire Trophy Race: Over 3,000 cc class	Sir J. Scott-Douglas	XK120
	Grand Prix de France, Rheims: Sports Car Race Over 2,000 cc class	S. Moss	C-type
	Jersey International Sports Car Race	I. Stewart	C-type
	International Alpine Rally: Over 3,000 cc class, *Coupe des Alpes, Alpine Gold Cup*.	E. I. Appleyard	XK120
1953	Tulip Rally, Holland: Touring Cars, 2,400-3,500 cc	E. I. Appleyard	Mk VII
	R.A.C. Rally: General classification	Mr. & Mrs. E. I. Appleyard	XK120
	Le Mans 24-Hour Race	A. P. R. Rolt/ J. D. Hamilton	C-type
	Rheims 12-Hour Race	S. Moss/ P. N. Whitehead	C-type

Date	Event and Class	Drivers	Model
1953	International Alpine Rally: Over 2,600 cc, *Coupe des Alpes*	Mr. & Mrs. E. I. Appleyard	XK120
	Greek Acropolis Rally: Overall winner	Papamichall	XK120
	Watkins Glen sports-car G.P., U.S.A.	W. Hansgen	XK120 Special
	Tourist Trophy Dundrod: 3,001-5,000 cc class	S. Moss/P. Walker	C-type
1954	Rheims 12-Hour Race	P. N. Whitehead/ K. Wharton	D-type
	Wakefield Trophy, Eire	P. Whitehead	Cooper-Jaguar
	Spa sports-car G.P., Belgium	H. Davids	C-type
	Coupe de Paris, Montlhéry	J. D. Hamilton	C-type
1955	Sebring 12-Hour Race	J. M. Hawthorn/ P. Walters	D-type
	Coupe de Paris, Montlhéry: Sports Car class	J. D. Hamilton	D-type
	Tulip Rally, Holland: Touring Cars, 2,600-3,500 cc	J. P. Boardman/ J. W. Whitworth	Mk. VII
	Ulster Trophy Race, Dundrod	J. D. Titterington	D-type
	Le Mans 24-Hour Race	J. M. Hawthorn/ I. L. Bueb	D-type
	Watkins Glen sports-car G.P., U.S.A.	S. Johnston	D-type
	Seneca Cup	M. R. J. Wyllie	C-type
1956	Monte Carlo Rally	R. Adams/F. Biggar	Mk VII
	Coupe de Paris, Montlhéry	J. D. Hamilton	D-type
	Belgian Production Car Races, Spa: Sports Car class	N. Sanderson	D-type
	Touring Car class	P. Frère	2.4 litre
	Rheims 12-Hour Race	J. D. Hamilton/ I. L. Bueb	D-type
	Le Mans 24-Hour Race	R. Flockhart/ N. Sanderson	D-type
	Watkins Glen sports-car G.P., U.S.A.	G. Constantine	D-type
1957	British Empire Trophy Race, Oulton Park	W. A. Scott-Brown	Lister-Jaguar
	Le Mans 24-Hour Race	R. Flockhart/ I. L. Bueb	D-type 3.8 litre
	Watkins Glen sports-car G.P., U.S.A.	W. Hansgen	D-type
1958	R.A.C. Rally: Production cars 2,001-2,600 cc	B. R. Waddilove/G. Wood	2.4 litre
	Production cars over 2,600 cc	E. N. Brinkman	3.4 litre
	Tulip Rally Holland: Series Production Cars, 2,000-2,600 cc	D. J. Morley/ G. E. Morley	2.4 litre
	Spa Sports Car G.P.	M. Gregory	Lister-Jaguar
	Bridgehampton Sports Car Race U.S.A.	W. Hansgen	Lister-Jaguar
1959	Tour de France: Touring category	Da Silva Ramos/ Estager	3.4 litre
	International Tulip Rally: General classification	D. Morley/E. Morley	3.4 litre
1960	International Alpine Rally: Touring car class	Behra/Richard	3.8 litre Mk II
	Tour de France: Touring car class	B. Consten/J. Renel	3.8 litre Mk II
	R.A.C. Rally: Touring Cars over 2,500 cc	J. Sears/W. Cave	3.8 litre Mk II
	Angola G.P., Africa	J. Love	D-type
1961	Tour de France: Touring Car class	B. Consten/J. Renel	3.8 litre

Date	Event and Class	Drivers	Model
1962	Nurburgring 6-Hour Touring Car Race	P. Lindner/P. Noecker	3.8 litre
	Nurburgring 12-Hour Touring Car Race	P. Lindner/H. J. Walter	3.8 litre
	Tour de France: Touring Car Class	B. Consten/J. Renel	3.8 litre
	Nurburgring 6-Hour Touring Car Race	P. Lindner	3.8 litre
1963	Tour de France: Touring Car Class	B. Consten/Renel	3.8 litre
	Coupe des Dames	Mlle. A. Soisbault/Mlle. L. Texier	3.8 litre
	Wills 6-Hour Touring Car Race, Pukehohe	A. Shelly/R. Archibald	3.8 litre
	Avus G.P., Berlin	P. Noecker	E-type
	International G.T. Race, Silverstone	G. Hill	E-type
	French G.P. Meeting, Rheims, Sports Car Race: G.T. car class	R. Protheroe	E-type
1963	European Touring Champion (Victories in Austria, Belgium, England, Germany & Hungary)	P. Noecker	3.8 litre
1964	Coupe de Paris Montlhéry G.T. Race	P. Sutcliffe	E-type
	International Australian G.P. Meeting: Touring Car Race	R. Jane	3.8 litre (bored-out) to 4.1 litre
	Spa, International Touring Car Race	C. Dubois	3.8 litre
1965	S. African G.P. Meeting, Sports/G.T. Race	P. Sutcliffe	E-type
	Wills 6-Hour Touring Car Race, Pukehohe, N.Z.	J. Ward/R. Coppins	3.8 litre
1966	Wills 6-Hour Touring Car Race, Pukehohe, N.Z.	A. Shelly/R. Archibald	3.8 litre
	Gran Premio Nacional, Bolivian Road Race	J. Burgoa	E-type

Since the mid-1960's Jaguar E-types have been consistently successful in G.T., Production Sports, and Modified Sports car club racing, but other Jaguar models have appeared only very rarely in competitions.

The 1933 Alpine Trial team according to the caption "outside the R.A.C.". Londoner's will know that it was down the road outside Marlborough House and — Marlborough spelt that way does not spell sponsorship!

One of the cars on an alpine pass — the driver is Margaret Allen who later married Christopher Jennings famous editor of the Motor. She is also the lone lady in the shot above.

Still the Alpine — and Charles Needham who won the award for the best individual performance. And enjoying a leisurely and perhaps even argumentative service Georg Hans Koch the Austrian SS importer.

Above: *S. H. Light at Monte Carlo where he won an award in the now defunct concours de confort.*
Centre: *Charles Needham on the Great St. Bernard in one of the later cars.*
low: *Before another "Monte" The Hon. Brian Lewis and a slightly apprehensive Lyons.*

Above: *The team which won the Welsh in 1937. Jacob, Rankin and Mathews.*

Centre: *A much modified SS 100 in the Stanley Cup race at the Crystal Palace. Driven by none other than a youthful George Abecassis.*

Below: *And equally youthful exuberance in a standard model at Prestcott in 1938.*

Above: *Mrs. "Bill" and Tommy Wisdom find time for a breather on the way to victory in "the Alpine"*

Centre: *"Old No. 8" re-appears with Wisdom at the wheel pretending to be Phi-Phi Etancelin.*

Below: *Ian Appleyard after his first (of many) Alpine win.*

Hardly a handy car for competition work the big Jaguars nevertheless they have done very well. Here are
Cotton and Didier, 4th overall in the '52 Monte.
Vard and Jolly (Mark V) in the '53 event
and Adams who won outright in 1954.

The 1955 Monte line-up cars commanded by Adams, Appleyard and Vard. Adams again in 1956. And even on the circuits. Appleyard leads Rolt at Silverstone (1954).

The start of the 1950 Le Mans with the white XK120 driven by Hadley — and a pit stop during the night with Leslie Johnson at the wheel. Johnson was very much in evidence at the wheel of the white XK in its early races.

Three shots of Stirling Moss at Dundrod in 1950 when he won the TT at 75.15 mph in the XK120 bearing his favourite number 7.

In August 1952 an XK120 coupé went to Montlhéry and captured a group of Class and World records. 72 hours, 4 days, 10,000 and 15,000 kms and 10,000 miles. Drivers seen here left to right were Johnson, Fairman and Hadley — Moss who also drove was

Left: *Improbable as it may look this XK120 Special of Walt Hansgen won the Watkin's Glen Grand Prix on September 19th 1953.*

Below: *Even more of a monster this bubble topped XK120 led development towards the E-type and covered the flying mile at 172.412 mph in 1953.*

Not so often remembered was the victory in the Liege-Rome-Liege in 1951. Drivers Jacquey Ickx (Senior) and band leader, Grand-Prix driver Johnny Claes.

Not intended as competitive cars the Mark II's (particularly 3.8's) had an astonishing success. Some of the races were little more than demonstrations particularly those at Silverstone. Seen here are Moss and below him one of the famous Sopwith/Hawthorn duels (Hawthorn No. 33) and lower still the 1963 German and European Champion.

Rallies continued to be fruitful — especially those incorporating some miles on racing circuits. An early 2.4 in front of a Chevrolet in the '59 Tulip and at the bottom of the page a saloon in the Alpine. Record breaking also continued. This Mark II did 10,000 miles at 106.58 mph at Monza mostly in the rain and returned a fuel consumption of 14 mpg while doing it.

On the other side of the world Tony Shelly and Ray Archibald win the New Zealand 6 hours for the 3rd time in 4 years and back in Europe Jaguar won the Touring Class in the Tour de France five times in a row. Here, in 1963 at Le Mans, is Costen in the lead.

No. 20, driven by Walker, leads away from the start at Le Mans in 1951 — behind are two Cunninghams. For the predictable outcome please turn over.

1951 saw the beginning of the immortal Jaguar victories at Le Mans. No. 20 driven by Walker and Whitehead claimed the honour and is here seen in the S at Arnage driven by Walker and at the bottom Whitehead takes the Winning Flag.

The success was almost unlimited from Le Mans to the TT (it's Moss again at Dundrod, above) on the British Circuits (this is Silverstone) and hill climbs everywhere in the hands of "pros" and amateurs alike.

*In 1953 the story continued according to plan.
Above: Ian Stewart No. 19. Moss (among
others!) on the pit counter and Hamilton at
the wheel and Rolt "on the pillion" the first
to win at over 100 mph and the first year
of disc brakes.
Opposite: The welcome home at Coventry
Council House.*

With the "bubble top" the original C/D prototype after records. Below: XKC005 seen at Oulton with Tony Wood. The car is ex-Wisdom and Moss and winner at Rheims (first time with disc brakes).

First appearance of the D-type at Le Mans two very famous cars, OKV 2 with Moss on left leaning across car to talk to Rolt, and OKV 1 with Rolt at the wheel during the race.

Le Mans again. Hawthorn in 55, a pit stop in 1956 with curious pyramid for non-existant passenger and a private XK140 still at it.

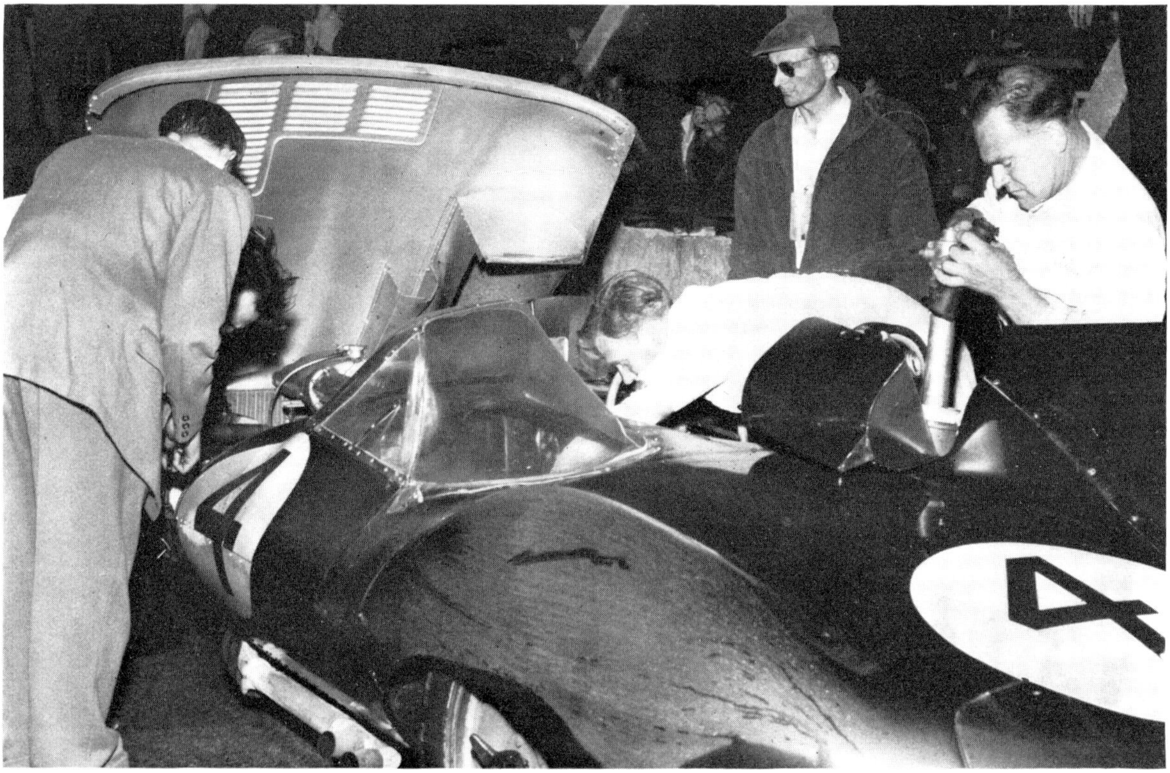

The final vistory at Le Mans, 1957, this time in the hands of Ecurie Ecosse. 3.8 long nose injection D-types with stripes across the nose for pits to identify drivers. Winner, with appropriately one stripe, was No. 3 in the hands of Bueb and Flockhart.

And here some specials. Goldie Gardner used the four cylinder XK engine in what used to be his MG special at Jabbeke in 1948, and Rivers Fletcher had a lot of fun with this Jaguar engined HWM which is still going strong.

Archie Scott Brown — one of the all time greats in the 1959 British Empire Trophy. The car is a Lister-Jaguar — and believe it or not this too is a Lister-Jaguar from the year before (1958). They came in all shapes as can be seen from the third example seen at Prestcott in 1961 driven by Phil Scragg.

When all the D-type fun was over the E-type soldiered on mostly in private hands. Seen here dominating the start at Oulton Park — as a lightweight version raced by Cunningham in 1963; and still much in evidence at Le Mans in 1964.

CHAPTER THIRTEEN

Acquisition

There is a well known saying in business that you cannot stay still — you must go forwards or backwards and from the first sidecar in Blackpool to the XK 120 at the 1948 Motor Show in London there was little doubt that Mr. William Lyons and his colleagues were going forward just about as fast as anyone in the industry. Indeed from time to time they must have felt rather like Alice in that it must have taken about all the running they could do to stay in the same place. But once the post-war company and its products were firmly established the need for expansion began to press.

The first move was in the direction of Daimlers, whose shadow factory the Company had already purchased. When, therefore, the need for further expansion was great and Lyons learned that "The Daimler" was for sale he entered into negotiations with Jack Sangster, who was then the Chairman of B.S.A., for the purchase of the Company. He recalls that it was a most amicable deal ending in a difference over a matter of £10,000 he recalls "Since each of us was honestly convinced that this was in our own favour, we decided that the only way to settle the matter was to toss-up for it. I am pleased to say that I won". Could the Gods possibly have allowed any other outcome?

So Jaguar bought Daimler — in a pretty run down state. They quickly put the good 2,500 cc Daimler V8 engine into the Mark II and made an excellent and very popular variant of that model. Later they used the Daimler range as an up-market version of the Jaguar which eventually included the Vanden Plas Limousine. The Daimler purchase also gave them a foothold in the bus business; and the later acquisition of Guy Motors brought them into trucks and big lorries as well. The important thing to note is that both these companies soon became very prosperous under the Lyons banner.

In 1963 they bought Coventry Climax, really a Company which should be thought of as successful in fire pumps and fork lift trucks; but one which all enthusiasts will think of as the firm whose engines completely dominated the Grand Prix scene for all the years they chose to make racing engines. This period was all but over by the time they became part of the Lyons empire; but there was one very significant detail in the person of Walter Hassan, who had left Jaguars to go to Coventry Climax, now returned to the fold and became Group Chief Engineer (Power Units).

A year later they made their final acquisition when they bought Henry Meadows of Wolverhampton, who were by then no longer concerned with the production of car engines — as they had been in the 'thirties when for example the famous 4½-litre Invicta used one of their power units; but were concerned with light engineering and the manufacture of Marine Gearboxes. The pack was then complete in itself.

After that Jaguar themselves became part of British Motor Holdings and finally the British Leyland Motor Corporation helping to create the second largest motor group outside America. As Sir William puts it himself "All this is a far cry from the 3 men and a boy with which this story began".

When Jaguar bought the Daimler Company they inherited a most interesting sports car in the SP250. Powered by a very neat V8 engine (seen Opposite*) it was available with a very good hard top — though it was not a beautiful car.*

It was popular with the police — these are London police models which it was thought could catch most people.
Below: *This car is not, as you might suppose a Reliant Scimitar, but an Ogle designed saloon on the SP250 Daimler chassis — from which the Reliant was developed later.*

Said by many to be at least as good as the contemporary Bentley the Daimler Majestic Major was also powered by a V8 engine. It was the choice of Lord Brabazon with appropriate number FLY 1. Below: The last of the old style Daimler limousines with the same $4\frac{1}{2}$ litre V8 as the Majestic Major.

Perhaps Jaguars most fascinating acquisition was Coventry Climax — and with them the return of Wally Hassan. Still dominating the Grand Prix scene under the old formula with the 4 valve V8 engine on the right.

Above: *Probably the greatest driver of all time Jim Clark in his Climax engined Lotus seen here at Silverstone.* Right: *One of the most complicated Grand Prix engines the Climax flat 16.*

With complete common sense one of the first things Jaguar did after buying Daimler was to put the 2½ litre V8 engine into the Mark II body to make a most interesting variant.

But after that Daimler became no more than a different radiator. Here the first "Sovereign" a Jaguar 420 by another name. There were, of course, minor differences of trim.

This is the current Daimler Limousine. The body is by Vanden Plas and a truly coachbuilt job but the dog beneath the skin is the "punt" of the Mark X or 420G if you prefer.

The Daimler version of the XJ6 — again called the Sovereign and again the same car with "up market" trimmings but still worthy of its ancient and honoured name.

Here are the Daimler versions of the XJ12 providing an opportunity to revive one of Daimlers greatest titles "The Double Six". Below: The long wheelbase model has wider rear doors and follows as you might expect the Jaguar in all essential details.

Taking a page from the British Leyland book Jaguar decided to take the Daimler Double Six one stage further — as had Austin before the days of the Princess. Vanden Plas re-made the interior of the car to their highest standards.

Outside they added a vynil roof and a real coachbuilder's paint job. With added chrome strip and a signature on the back panel making a truly enviable machine — long wheelbase versions were also available.

As with the Jaguar, the Series Two Daimler Sovereign and Double Six have a revised front end and slightly cleaned up rear. Above: The Double Six in two door form. Below: The now standard long wheelbase version, the shorter wheelbase Double Six, four door saloon having been discontinued.

CHAPTER FOURTEEN

Personalities and Permutations

One of the great joys of collecting photographs for a volume of this nature, is the number of pictures that turn up and resolutely refuse to fit into ordinary chapter headings. In this case they are mostly of men or of machines which have some special significance as part of the Jaguar tradition — they are not always connected, and yet the thread of the Jaguar story binds them all together. Most of the men are engineers and other members of Sir William's team without whom, as he has always been the first to say, things would not have been what they are. Others from Clark Gable to Ian Appleyard are people whose interest in the car, though quite varied, has played a largish part in the creation of the image.

On the mechanical side there are some prototype engines which never became Jaguars at all and the XJ13, the splendid mid V12 engined machine, destined to be nothing more than a high speed test-bed after a change in Le Mans regulations and company policy, some interesting uses of the existing engines, in cars and boats, which go to show that there is more to the heart of a Jaguar than just another Jaguar. And then there are the acquisitions in which men and machines meet; together with a reminder that though roads may be widened and backgrounds change old soldiers never die, and indeed given the chance don't even fade away.

Sir William's post war export success to the United States was helped more than a little by the interest of the famous. He is here seen in California with one of his most famous and most consistant customers Clark Gable.

In Europe much of Jaguars competition success was, for some five years after the war, largely in the hands of Ian Appleyard seen here with his two mounts. Appleyard was the Yorkshire distributor for Jaguars for many years and at one time married to Sir William's daughter.

Not, as today's image might suggest, a takeover by the Mafia, but Capt. Strickland, M.P. for Coventry (Centre) bidding goodbye to SS cars sole concessionaire in the U.S., one Richard G. Taylor. Bill Rankin looks on. Knowing your own product. At Donnington in an SS Rally, left to right Bill Heynes, Sammy Newsome and Bill Lyons. Elizabeth Taylor and husband (at that time) Michael Wilding following Gable's footsteps.

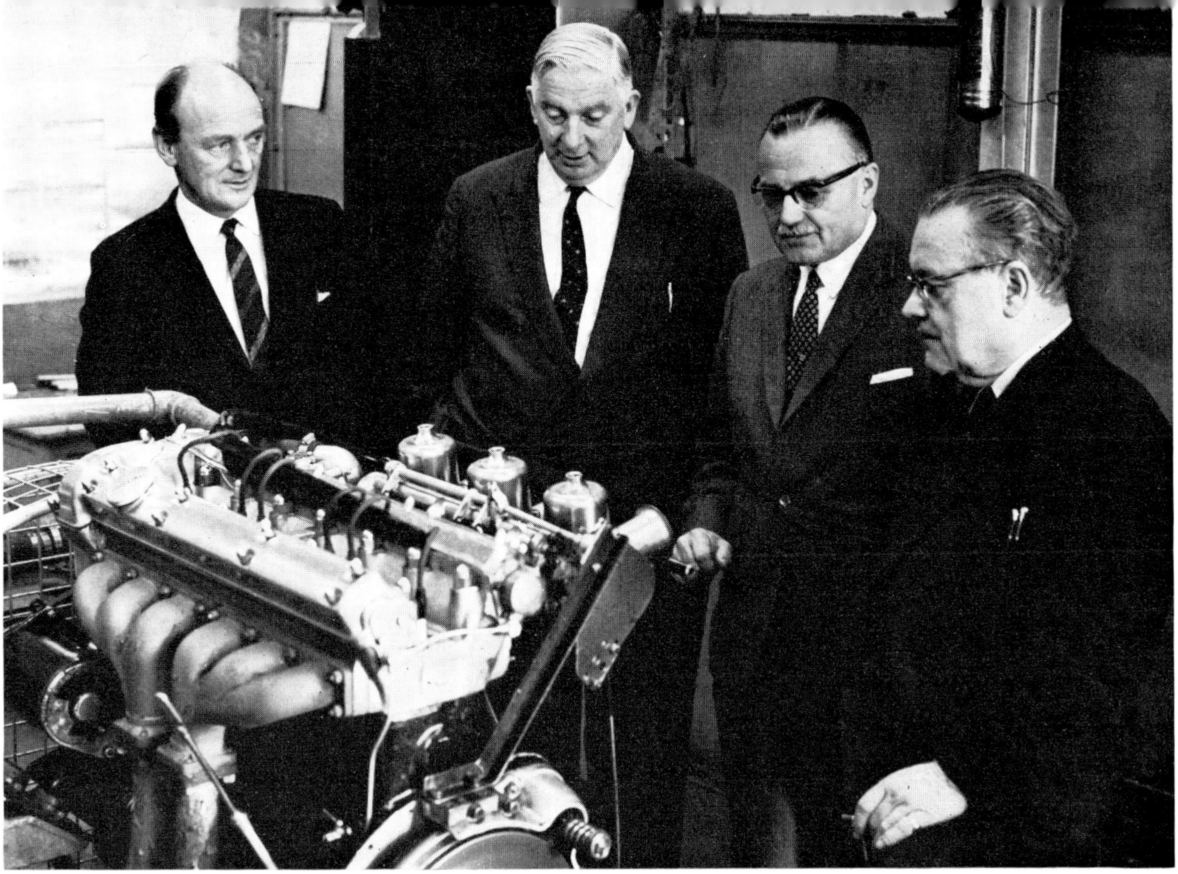

The engineering "greats". Above: *With an XK6 Mundy, Hassan, Heynes and Baily (Chief engine designer — Jaguar).* Below: *With the 16 cylinder Climax, Lee (of Climax) and Hassan.*

Stages in the development of the XK series which began as can be seen in the SS days.

XF

XG

XK

Two recent examples of the XJ6. Above: *The three carburettor version fitted in an E-type.* Below: *An example with emission control cross over for the American market.*

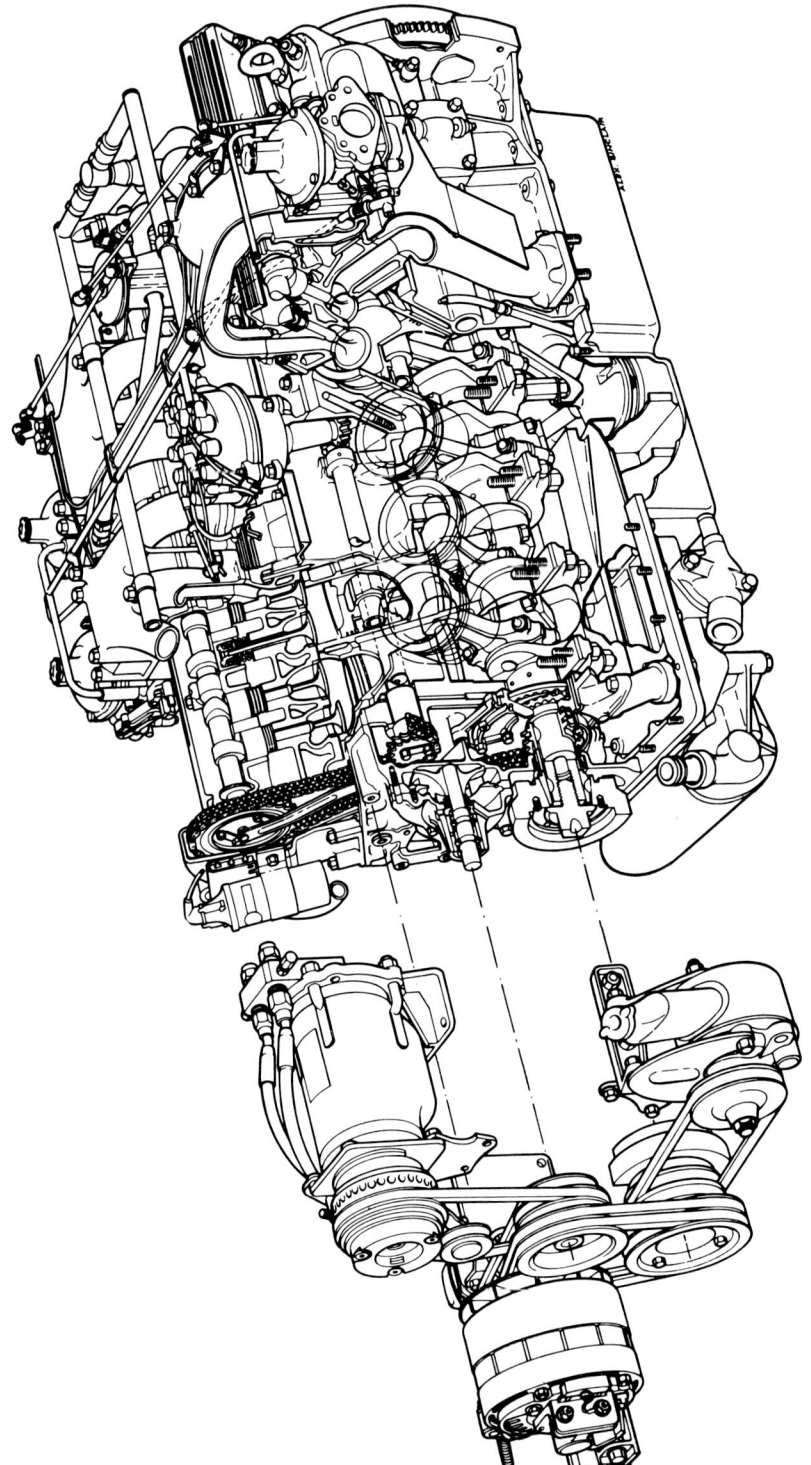

An exploded view of the present XJ12 with one overhead camshaft and two carburettors per block of 6 cylinders. It can be compared with the twin-cam V12 on the opposite page.

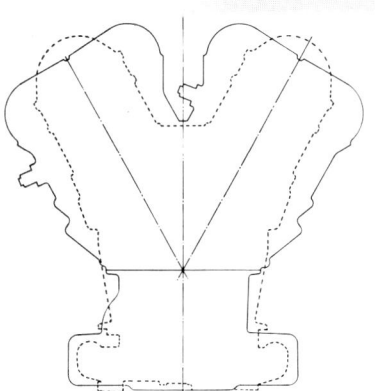

Above: *The twin-cam V12 which was fitted to the XJ13 (overleaf).* Left: *A silhouette comparison between the single and twin camshaft engines which goes some way to explain the eventual choice of the latter — seen in the photograph below.*

The XJ13 as it is today, rebuilt after a shunt and demonstrated at the British Grand Prix in 1973. It is in almost all respects as it was before but those with an eye for detail will notice that the tyres are now wide and the wheel arches are more substantial.

This is the XJ13 as it originally was in the mid-1960's. Planned but never used to defend Jaguars honour at Le Mans. The sudden, and to many, stupid changes in the regulations made the company abandon its interest. On the banking at MIRA it is driven by tester Norman Dervis and the engine can be better seen on page 201.

Jaguars have always had a good market with the police — for reasons of both prestige and performance. The shot on the opposite page is not in fact a still from a Terry Thomas film but a scene from life, in Fiji; although dated 1937 the Jaguar sticker on the screen makes that improbable, as evidenced by the British car above. Even the women got into the act with the Mark II.

Two Daimler pictures of more than passing interest. Below: *Sammy Davis and Monty Tonks both late of the Autocar and both once Daimler apprentices with a Daimler Sovereign just by the works.* Above: *The same spot in 1914 with the then current Daimler chassis on test.*

What's in a name one might well ask but more interesting would be to know what's in a number plate since none of them appear to be British. The two cars by the Jaguar fighter are Series I E-types, the first with "open" lamps.

The XK engine has done nearly as well afloat as ashore. Weber carburettors were used by Von Mayenhag for his record breaking Mathea VII. While British enthusiasts will know the many successes achieved by Norman Buckley in his Miss Windermere III.